Relationship Break Up Survival Guide

By: Pete Taylor M.A., LCPC

Trafford rev. 09/27/2011

 www.trafford.com

North America & international
toll-free: 1 888 232 4444 (USA & Canada)
phone: 250 383 6864 ♦ fax: 812 355 4082

Many thanks to Meffy, without you this book would never have been possible to write. You helped me in ways that you don't even know.

Thanks too to my parents, Matthew and Marion, who showed me in an up close and personal way what a healthy relationship is, and how to maintain it.

PREFACE

So you picked up this book for a reason, and that reason is that you are looking for some assistance in surviving a relationship break up. My friend, you have made a good decision—but don't stop here—do yourself a favor and read the entire book. If you take to heart what I have written, you will begin to feel better, begin to see that there is life and light at the end of the tunnel, and you will begin to see that happiness and the joy that once was can be had again.

The road to renewal does not come without its share of work…. hard work….but you can do it. So let's take the journey together—it is not a long tedious journey—who wants to go through that? If we wanted a long tedious, painful journey we'd just let time pass and nature take it's course…..What we want is to minimize the pain and hard feelings—quickly--and this book was written with that in mind….Just take a look at it—it is a thin, easy to read, easy to understand hand book that is written in plain English…. I want to escort you on a short, intense journey designed to get you back on your feet again, smiling again, and confident again…happy again… and it is written by someone that has been in your shoes—but chose to do something about it……

If you want to know more about me, you can read my biography on the internet. Sure, I am a licensed, clinical, professional counselor

that has his Masters Degree in psychology blah blah blah……..
Who cares what my credentials are—most importantly, I have been through relationship break ups and have applied the principles in this book to help me get my life back on track and minimize the pain that a break up can cause…not to mention the heartache, lost concentration and productivity on the job, reduction in self esteem, feelings of depression and worthlessness, isolation, and even suicidal thoughts. So if you're feeling any of the above—or all of the above, stick with me and we'll move forward together….

As a counselor though, I have to state, for the record, that this book in no way should be used as a replacement for psychiatric or psychological care or therapy. If you're currently seeing a mental health professional, continue seeing them. If you do not have a therapist or counselor, you may want to consider finding one to help you in addition to the information in this book… If you need to consult a therapist to assist you through the recovery process—by all means do so—at the very least, email me and I can refer you to one in your town…Your mental health is what we're trying to restore, and that is paramount on the list of priorities…Right now, though, I don't want to waste any time—let's jump in and get started…..

I am going to break down the steps in surviving a relationship break up into easy to read chapters. Each chapter will cover a specific suggestion for you to follow to get you back to feeling good again. Each chapter is important in its own right—but each chapter may not be for everyone. Use the chapters that work for you. If every chapter works for you, fantastic! Most of them should at least provide you with something to consider and possibly apply.…I can tell you right away that every suggestion might not sit well with you---but I am asking you to keep an open mind and just try it. What have you got to lose? You will notice right away that each chapter is short, and easy to get through. Don't just read the title of the chapter and assume that it is not for you…Come on, no short cuts here—the book is short enough…read the chapter (in many cases they are only a page in length!) then decide if it is a principle that you want to apply. Part of the beauty of this book is that it is quick, easy and effective. I have written it with shortcuts already in place!

Everyone that has been in a relationship most likely has suffered through a break up. Most everyone has their own way of dealing with it…this book is not written for any specific age group, gender or sexual identity. Anyone can use and apply the principles outlined here. I am not going to go as far as to say we will apply tough love on you—but I will go as far as to say there are no excuses—you've got the book, you know how to read—let's go!

So are you game? Can you hold true to the two things that I am asking of you? Can you keep an open mind and try the principles outlined in the next thirty pages or so? If you can't then do us both a favor—take the book back to the bookstore and ask for a refund. If you can, then keep on reading and take heart in the fact that you are on the quickest road to recovery from a broken heart that I can think of—and I can say this because I have practiced these techniques and they work. So fasten your seat belts, tighten your chinstrap, here we go…………………

CHAPTER ONE

"Cry"

I know what you're probably thinking....you are probably thinking, "What the heck? I just paid a handful of bucks for this book—and this author is telling me to cry?!"

Ok, not exactly a recommendation that would ever get confused with therapeutic advice or rocket science...but too many times people try to survive a break up by *not* crying...Too many times people try to survive a relationship break up by being tough—and gutting it out...You *need* to cry sometimes. When someone you love dies, when your dog runs away, or when you break up with someone you love, you need to cry.

You can make up your own mind if you want to cry at sad movies or not. You can make your own mind as to whether to cry or not when your pet goldfish dies...I am not here to judge—but I am here to tell you that when you break up with someone it is a loss—a devastating loss--and crying helps to express your feelings and helps get it out of your system.

Crying alone will not eradicate the hurt and pain, but it will help a great deal. Crying helps by the mere expression of your emotions. Holding back the tears just keeps the hurt and pain inside of you – and it can take root if it stays inside of you for too long…. So don't fight it. Cry when the feeling hits you—and don't hold back. Let the tears flow. Now, I am not suggesting that you do this while at your computer monitor at work or while you are in line at the grocery store—but when you are alone and by yourself and the feeling hits you—let it all hang out.

Crying cleanses the soul……ok, that was corny. But in a way it is true—and it does. When you cry it releases emotions in a way that speaking or yelling our emotions just cannot.

When you are feeling the pain and hurt connected to the person that you used to be in a relationship with, a deeper outpouring of emotions is necessary at times in order to dig to the deepest levels of your being, reach down and grab that pain, and shove it out of your body…Crying does just that. Those **tears are your pain and hurt**—and they are coming from the very depth of your heart—**you need to let them out** in order to move on.

So try it! Let yourself feel the pain……let the tears come down…….Allow yourself to be free with this emotion—at least for a little while. It is the first step towards feeling better. The world has got enough tough guys (and girls)—we don't need one more---if you're feeling pain, let it out---let the tears flow…you will be better for it….

This crying thing may hit you when you least expect it…You may hear a familiar song on the radio, or you pass by a familiar landmark, or you watch a sad movie—ordinarily you may not cry at the thought of these things alone…but if these things begin to make you cry after your break up—again, don't fight it—the tears are probably connected to the pain and the hurt of the break up and it will be healthier for you to let the tears begin…

CHAPTER TWO

"Give it some time"

You've heard the phrase, "Give it some time….it will be all right", right? Well, it's easy to tell someone to "Give it some time" when you're not the one with a broken heart…So if someone tells you to "give it some time, you'll be all right" try to refrain from punching them—I am sure they mean well…

With this said, giving things some time is actually sound advice… because time does help to ease the pain and suffering. Time doesn't stand still—and when you break up with someone, time may seem to drag on very slowly, but it really *doesn't* stand still.

Here's the key to 'giving it some time'…USE YOUR TIME WISELY.

Many people have survived relationship break ups…it isn't easy, and for some, it is downright miserable….but what happens to the ones that have the 'downright miserable' experience? Time passes and they survive. That is where the 'give it some time' theory came from. Breaking up with someone usually is not fatal—even though it feels like it can be. We survive these break ups over time—but who wants to suffer needlessly or longer than they have to!?

That is why I say to "Use your time wisely"…time spent after a break up is some of the toughest time spent in a person's life…the emotional depths can be crippling. That is why I wrote this book— and by using your time wisely you can minimize the length of time (and possibly the intensity) spent in a crippled emotional state.

So, with all of this "Give it some time" thought on our minds, in this chapter I want to discuss one major point related to time and what to do with it after a break up…

The tendency after a break up is to focus on negatives…I refer to this as focusing on "the loss"…This is normal—and necessary—the only problem with this is that it is (can be) terribly painful, and it doesn't move us forward at all…so if focusing on the loss is necessary and normal, but it doesn't move us forward, (not to mention that it is painful) what do we do?

The answer to this question is that we have to allow ourselves to wallow or focus on the loss, but **limit the amount of time that we engage in it**. Wallowing is like a pity party that we throw for ourselves…and, if we are to be honest with ourselves, it feels good to do so…Problem is, when things feel good we tend to want to do them over and over again---wallowing and self-pity feel good and can be habit forming. Remember when I said that wallowing doesn't move us forward? This is the dangerous part of wallowing – it is necessary in the process of surviving a relationship break up--it feels good but can be habit forming—and we get absolutely nowhere by doing it for prolonged periods of time…

So, here's what I need you to do—and this takes some self-discipline: When you get the urge to feel sorry for yourself—go ahead and do it. That's right, I said go ahead and do it—allow yourself to wallow.…BUT limit the amount of time that you allow yourself to do it…and the amount of time may change each time you feel the need – sometimes it may be a few hours, some times you might only need ten minutes…but set a clear timetable for when you plan to stop the wallowing…I mean this quite literally—I want you to say (or think) to yourself: "I will allow myself to wallow until eleven o'clock" (or whatever time you decide), and really let yourself be 100% committed to wallowing for that allotted period of time. But when eleven o'clock comes around, you have to give up the exclusive wallowing and involve yourself in something else… that something else may involve some wallowing—but it won't be exclusive wallowing after your time is up…

For example: You wake up one morning and you just feel overwhelmed with emotions, pain and hurt…you may even allow yourself to cry a bit and let some of that pain and hurt out….your thoughts are probably revolving around the pain and hurt and how the loss is affecting your life…these thoughts are tough to stop—and no one is suggesting that you can—I am merely saying to limit the time that you allow these types of thoughts to be your absolute primary focus.

Setting time limits for wallowing can be tough to follow and it may take some practice…but really try. The first few times you try this you may have to extend your time limits because wallowing is hard to stop…you may also have to have several "wallowing times" during the day for a while…this is ok, but keep practicing (and utilizing the suggestions in this book) and you will find that it will become easier and easier the more you try it…

The self-discipline you will be practicing will also give you a sense of control in a situation in which you may have perceived you had no control at all---and that is a very good thing! Because you have more control than you might think in this situation—you just need to exercise it—**setting time limits for wallowing is a good way to exercise some control, practice self control and develop confidence in the fact that you have more control than you think!**

CHAPTER THREE

"Express Yourself"

There used to be an old song that had the words, "Express yourself" in the chorus…I don't have the slightest idea who sang it—but the message was to express yourself and let your emotions out…that is the focus of this chapter…

Just as crying is a way of getting your emotions out, so is expressing yourself---and there are many ways of doing this…not all of the ones listed below may suit you—but find one that you can use and do it, you will feel better for the effort…

Why is expressing yourself important? Great question—it's important because just as crying lets out some of the pain and hurt from deep within us, so does expressing ourselves in other ways… Plus, we need a variety of ways to express ourselves because we might look a little silly if all we do is go around crying all the time!

Talking/Venting: Talk to your friends about how you are feeling…if they are truly your friends, they will listen…they may want to give you advice—tell them you've already bought a book that is helping you with that—and that you just need them to listen…Having an ear that you can turn to when you need someone to hear you is vital...just make sure that you are talking to or venting to someone that has the compassion to actually listen to not just your words but to your *feelings*...and for you guys reading this—yes I said "Feelings" – it is not a dirty word— you don't have to use all types of flowery words as long as 'how you're feeling' comes through in the words you *do* use...

Now you don't want to over burden your friends by expressing your feelings to them ad nauseum , but that is what friends are for— to listen to us when we need them to...check in with them every now and again by asking them if they are still ok with listening— and let them know that you are grateful for their patience and understanding...it is at these times that we really need our friends and we don't want to jeopardize their support by leaning too heavily on them...

Writing/Journaling: If you are a writer or someone that keeps a journal, use this talent to get your feelings out and on paper...any type of expression is helpful in getting the hurt and pain out of our system. Don't hold back here—write out everything that you are feeling...use whatever type of language you care to—if four letter words help you express what pain or hurt you feel, then by all means, use them...just keep your journal away from small children!

One word of caution here: You may be tempted to write a letter, email, text message, or some other form of correspondence to the person that you broke up with...this can be tricky. I am not advocating harassing anyone – and if the correspondence is unwanted, your contact can possibly be construed as such...So write out your feelings but you may want to consult with a close friend as to whether to share your written feelings with the object of your pain and hurt...

I believe you will find that merely writing your feelings out will suffice in helping to ease the hurt, and getting it out of your system—provided you follow the other suggestions in this book...

if your "ended relationship" lends itself to mutual contact—and you can keep your written expression of your feelings appropriate and respectful—then by all means go for it and send off that letter or email...just don't expect much in return...this is where it gets tricky...by maintaining contact with the person that broke up with you it could prolong the hurt and pain because you will be continuing to expose yourself to the agent of the pain...so be careful here...

My writing this book is an example of 'expressing myself' and getting my emotions out...writing can be very therapeutic—and you don't have to pay a counselor or lie down on a couch to get the benefits!

Let your creative juices flow: Do you sing? Paint? Create arts and crafts? Write poetry? Play guitar or some other musical instrument? Design clothes? Do you do anything that can be construed in the slightest bit as being creative? If so, do it! Do it a lot! Do it some more! Do it until you're sick of doing it! Your emotions will come out in your work and it won't seem like work at all!

If you are a writer, get to your keyboard and just let the words come out...same for a painter—get to the canvass and break out the paint...Art therapists make a living by interpreting the creative work of those that are hurting in some way—they do it by analyzing the work of their patients or clients....These therapists believe that our emotions come through in the work that is created—rather unconsciously—so by letting your creative juices flow you will be helping yourself by getting your emotions out and you may not even realize it! That is the beauty of art therapy (or any other creative outlet – it is therapy for many of us!)

If you play a musical instrument – grab it and begin playing... just like art therapy there is music therapy...yes, you got it—your emotions will come out in the music you play—and just like other creative outlets, you might not even realize it...

Music: Listen to it! Get your favorite CD's and take them with you in your car, put them in your stereo system at home and let the music move you…if you want to listen to songs that describe heartache, that's ok….just make sure that when you are done it is helping you to get your feelings out instead of magnifying them (you will know the difference)…Sing along with those heartbreak songs—this can be very therapeutic—it might not be very good for the neighbors—but who cares?! This is all about you for right now… they'll get over it! Remember, it is all about getting those emotions out—who cares if you cannot carry a tune---who can hear you when you are in your car? Who can hear you when you are in your shower? Get the point? Get those feelings out! CREATE and EXPRESS!

Chapter Four

"Do for others"

This may be the easiest of all chapters to write…and if you're with me this far, congratulations! This may be the chapter that you get the most out of…

So what do I mean when I say 'do for others'? It is simple really…when you have a broken heart, it is very easy to fall into the trap of self-centeredness…Everything becomes "Woe is me" and all of your attention is on you. It's no secret—and don't feel badly about it—it is just human nature…and that is ok…….you deserve all of the attention when your heart is breaking. But we are not into holding onto the pain and hurt, we are about overcoming the pain and hurt and moving forward---so if you continue your self-centered ways, it will be much more difficult to move forward and it will take a lot more time and energy.

This is why we say to 'time limit' your self-pity…if you don't you can drown in it, and as a result never get beyond it.

So, how do we shift the focus of our own attention from ourselves to others? Great question—a great question that has lots of answers…I cannot possibly write all of the options here in this book and keep it short, sweet and easy to read—so you may have to come up with some ideas of your own...but I will get you started with a few...

But before I do, I have to remind you of the two things I asked of you way back at the beginning of the book: "Keep an open mind and try it"...some of my suggestions may not seem like a good fit for you—but keep an open mind and try some of them—you may find that they work! If not, come up with your own ideas – but apply yourself—**don't just think about it, do it**!

The benefits of doing for others is three-fold:

1. When you do for others it takes the focus off of you, allowing you to escape the trap of self-pity and wallowing...
2. When you do for others it makes you feel very good inside. It makes you feel worthwhile and valuable. Aren't those the feelings that you lost when the break up occurred? It is a wonderful feeling to get those back—even if it is in a totally different arena than a relationship—trust me on this!
3. When you do for others, the "others" that you are doing for are benefiting...a triple bonanza of good!

Ok, enough blabber on my part—here are some ideas as to how you can apply the principle of "Doing for others":

A) Go through your closet and pull out all of your old clothes—put them in a hefty bag or an old plastic blue shopping bag and donate them to the nearby homeless shelter. Don't just drop them in one of those metal boxes on the side of the road—go to the shelter and donate them—see the people you'll be helping...it will make you feel better...and they will appreciate you for your efforts—you cannot get that from a metal box!

This may require a little planning to find out where the nearest shelter is, their hours of operation, do they accept donations etc. So don't be lazy here—do the little bit of legwork that it will take to get this done...

B) Do the same things in letter "A" above, but do it with food from a grocery store...call up the shelter (look up the number in the phone book or internet) and ask them what they could use. Do they need rice or bread? Maybe cereal or ground beef...whatever they need, buy a bit of it and go and deliver it! You have just helped to feed people that otherwise may have gone hungry—that has got to make you sleep better! And it has got to make you feel worthwhile and valuable as a person.

C) Call the shelter and ask if they need help serving meals... you can go in and serve a meal each week and it won't cost you anything but your time...homeless shelters always need help with this kind of thing....

OK, Homeless shelters not your thing?—too uncomfortable for you or too scary? (Really no reason to be scared – the residents are people just like you and me!) Here are some more ideas—but I hope you are keeping to the two things I asked of you here—keep an open mind...great!

D) Buy a bag of groceries—doesn't have to be anything that will break you, and bring them to the local food bank or church...the food bank always needs food for the needy, and the church can always find a family that can use food...

E) Ok, buying things might not be your thing—what talent have you got? Can you cut the grass for free at the local ball field?

F) How about help a neighbor paint his house or take out his trash if he has difficulty lifting heavy things?

G) If it is wintertime and you get snow where you live, can you help someone clean the snow off of his or her car?

H) Maybe you can go visit elderly residents at an assisted living facility—they would be delighted to see you!

You get the idea---do for others—it has so many benefits! No one has to know that you are doing it to help you through your break up—that can be our secret. In the end you will be helping others and that makes the world a better place—and it makes us feel better about ourselves in the process. That too makes the world a better place!

Refreshing those feelings inside of us that scream: "I am worthwhile!" and "I am lovable!" and "I like who I am!" and "I feel good about me!".....this is important—and what better way to refresh these feelings than through helping others...trust me (I know I have used this phrase several times) it works!

Before we move onto the next chapter, it is worth mentioning that when I suggest "Doing for others" it doesn't always have to be major things like volunteering or purchasing some type of goods to donate....Try the little things first, like saying "Good morning" to the people in the elevator on your way to work, or as you are getting your morning coffee, hold the door open for the next person entering the seven eleven behind you...

Small acts of kindness will have the same effects on your psyche as the larger things you do—and the little things can be done all throughout the day....the end result is that after you practice these acts of kindness you will feel good about who you are and that will increase your feelings of self worth...when we feel better about ourselves we act better as individuals towards others and we attract good things to us....(and this, by the way, helps take the attention away from our hurt and pain, and that is always a good thing!)

CHAPTER FIVE

"Choose a mantra"
and
"Look towards a higher power"

Ok, nice job so far—you've made it this far...let's keep going. This chapter is very important—it will make a huge difference in your ability to continue moving forward positively. As with the other chapters, keep an open mind and give it a try...this is a two part chapter because I know the minute I mention a "Higher Power" some of you will immediately get turned off and think that I am about to lay a twelve step program on you. Relax, I am not. I also realize that some of you out there are also jazzed about the mentioning of a "Higher Power" because you have believed in one the entire time—and probably have been leaning on one to keep from going crazy through this break up.

In either case-hear me out through this chapter, and if at the end of the next few pages you don't think it was helpful, well then, what have you lost except the time it took to read a couple of pages...right? Great...I appreciate your willingness...I knew there was something I liked about you!

One of the biggest problems of trying to survive and thrive after a relationship break up is that the majority of our thoughts when it comes to the person we broke up with are negative, hurtful or hostile. This type of thinking is detrimental to our mental health. Some of you are asking yourself right now, "How is that detrimental to my mental health?". Here's how:

By thinking negative things about the person that broke up with us we are stopping the healthy process of moving forward. We cannot effectively move forward while thinking negatively. It is impossible. Those that continue to think negative things about their ex become prisoners of their own thoughts….**thinking negative things about our ex in the end makes us feel bad about ourselves**—because we (deep down) don't want to be a negative person—yet that is what most of us become. The ironic part of this is that we think negative thoughts (e.g. 'She's no good' or 'She never loved me' or worse) about our ex to make ourselves feel better, and in reality it has the opposite affect on us---we feel worse about ourselves in the long run. Oh, sure it makes us feel better for a brief while—dragging our ex down into the muddy depths—but the long term effects on us are damaging—because we become this negative, bad mouthing person that we really don't like ourselves to be. I hope this makes sense—if it doesn't, re-read the last paragraph and let it sink in---it is that important!

So how do we combat the urges to think or say bad, derogatory things about our ex, especially when we are hurting and view them as the causal agent of that hurt and pain? It takes self-discipline and a good mantra. "A good mantra?" you ask? Yes, a good mantra… This mantra will be a phrase that you will think to yourself or say out loud every time you think about your ex….this is where the self discipline comes in---you will be very tempted to think or say something negative---fight the urge!!! And instead recite your mantra! Choose something that you can actually feel good about… Below are some examples—but make sure you choose something short, sweet and that fits you…

Examples of positive mantras that you can use whenever you think about your ex and are tempted in thinking something negative:

1. I wish the best for her (or him)
2. I want nothing but good things for her (or him)
3. We had some very good times and I am grateful
4. I wish her (or him) well
5. I pray for the best for her (or him)
6. I hope he (or she) is doing well

These mantras might not be easy to execute right off the bat—you may still be too angry or upset—this is why this is not the first chapter in this book! We have to work our way up to being able to wish good things for our ex—this, in fact, does take time…but the sooner you can get to this point the quicker your survival will materialize…

The beauty of this strategy is that instead of thinking negative things about our ex that act as road blocks to our own mental health—these types of mantras actually make ourselves feel better about ourselves, and help to restore the feelings that we are missing--dignity, self-esteem, self-worth etc…This happens because we perceive ourselves taking the high road in the break up…we are being a good person—being the better person—being the person we like seeing ourselves be--this does make a difference!

So where does the belief in a "Higher Power" come into play? Well, it is sometimes easier to pray for the other person as part of the mantra or as a bedtime ritual—this not only accomplishes the task of helping us feel better about who we are in the moment—but also assists with helping us sleep more easily because it decreases the tendency for our minds to race with negativity during times like these…

Plus, belief in a "Higher Power" gives us the option of praying for our own strength to hold true to the principles that you are reading about now...to pray for help in being able to stand tall and to carry out the suggestions in these chapters gives us another source of support in a time when we need all the support that we can get...

So practice your mantra—over and over again...and then when you have those urges of negativity towards your ex, break out the mantra and repeat it several times until it sinks in...practice it until it becomes second nature...it will eventually—and feel yourself feeling good about 'taking the high road' when it comes to your thought process...You will actually begin to feel those emotions coming back into your being---and once you get a taste of that you won't want to stop...

And do you know why you won't want to stop? Because you will begin to perceive yourself as having some control over your thoughts---no longer will they be in control of you—flooding you with negativity—dragging you down further into a pit of low self-esteem....instead you will be lifting yourself up in a wave of positive mantras—all the while regaining control over your thoughts and feelings---and your survival!

Chapter Six

"Look inside yourself"

How often do we ask ourselves, "What could I have done differently?" Now ask yourself, "Have I asked that same question about the break up?" You probably have—but I don't want you to think of the answer in the traditional sense—I want you to think of what you could have done differently from within...Inside the depths of your being—what could you have done differently?

This is a good time for self evaluating---because if you don't do a bit of self evaluation, you may be bound to make the same mistakes in your next relationship as you did in this past one...and we don't want to have to re-live the pain and hurt...

So let the evaluation begin....were you the best person you could be within the realm of the relationship? Were you as considerate, thoughtful, courteous, or respectful? I want you to learn from the mistakes of the past but this will require a great deal of honesty on your part...I am a licensed, clinical, professional counselor, but I don't want to counsel you in this chapter—I want you just to look inside yourself, be truthful, and identify what unhealthy things you brought to the last relationship and take ownership of them.

Once you do this – believe it or not- you will feel better about being up front with the person that counts most---YOU!

What are some of the possible unhealthy behaviors that you may have been guilty of bringing into the last relationship? Below is a short list of some of the most common:

1. Being controlling
2. Acting jealous
3. Selfishness with your time, energy and attention
4. Disrespectful
5. Demeaning in the way you treated her (or him) or the things you said to her (or him)
6. Doing things that dragged the relationship down instead of building each other up
7. Non supportive of their goals
8. Putting them down and making them feel stupid or small
9. Showing attention towards other people in a romantic way – making your partner feel unworthy
10. Being violent or physically or mentally abusive in any way
11. Being inconsiderate of their feelings, wishes or dreams
12. Not listening to them when they wanted to share
13. Not sharing your own feelings, thoughts and dreams

If you were a party to acting I any of the listed ways—you must admit it to yourself and own the behaviors…in order to move forward you must confront yourself and agree to work on these areas – not for your next relationship sake—but for your sake! By improving yourself and becoming a better person you can begin to feel good about who you are and how you behave—and this is a huge part of surviving a break up---you NEED to feel better about yourself—but you cannot feel better about yourself if you have been a person that doesn't behave and treat your significant others well…

So own those unhealthy behaviors and vow to do something about them...

What can you do about them? If you cannot change on your own, then enlist the assistance of a counselor or therapist.....ask your friends if they think you could stand to improve in the areas you've identified—if they are your real friends they will probably say 'yes' – then ask them if they are willing to help you by pointing out when you might act this way in the future...this can be helpful—and really good friends will help you...

Just identifying the behaviors and being honest will have a positive affect on you—and then taking the first step towards changing will make you feel even better----and in the long run when you are in a healthier place emotionally, you will be more prepared to enter a healthy relationship and less likely to repeat the same mistakes that have contributed to this most recent break up...

Good luck – this past chapter can be tough...but I know that you can do it!

CHAPTER SEVEN

"Seek out your friends"

We mentioned friends in the last chapter and we're not finished with them yet...in this chapter I want you to seek them out and do things with them....

Too many times we enter into a relationship, and the next thing we know is that we begin to lose contact with our friends because we are with our partner all the time...this happens to a lot of us once we get 'involved' with someone. It is not until we break up that 'someone' that we begin to seek out our friends...This is normal, so don't wait around too long—seek them out.

If you've got your mantra working, and you doing for others, and you are getting your feelings out—the next step is to stay active... Depression is the result of inactivity. You need to get out and do something—surround yourself with people that are supportive of you and that like you. Hopefully – your friends like you! Call them even if you have to force yourself to pick up the phone—call them and ask them to do something with you—don't sit and wallow!

I am not asking you to go out and start scoping out potential replacements for your lost love—just go out and stay busy. An idle mind is an active mind – and right now your thoughts are prone to negativity...so we don't want your mind to be too active! So keep it occupied and don't forget your mantra!

So how do we do this? What if all of our friends are hooked up with boyfriends or girlfriends? That really sucks being a third wheel!

Ok, been there done that...third wheel nights are lousy, I admit—but no one says that you have to settle for being a third wheel---you have more control over this than you may realize-there are lots of things you can do to get out there and be active:

1. Join a bowling league
2. Play bingo
3. Join a singles club or dating site
4. Join a co-ed sports league and play volleyball or softball or flag football
5. Volunteer at a community based program to help people in need
6. Volunteer at an animal shelter
7. Volunteer anywhere!
8. Join a support group
9. Start a support group

CHAPTER EIGHT

"Practice rituals if you need to"

What the heck do I mean by "practice rituals"? This means that you can use some rituals or specific activities designed to burn lasting thoughts into your brain that will assist you through your struggles. These thoughts are specifically purposed to replace nagging thoughts that may be holding you back or dragging you down...Rituals are used to help people get over loss---and the relationship that has broken up is a loss...

The idea is to choose a ritual to assist you in forgetting something bad that has happened to you---or to ease the pain and hurt of something negative that has occurred in your life...The break up is the something bad—and the pain and hurt is what we are trying to get rid of by using the ritual---and a ritual is just an activity that provides a memory that is easy to hold onto that can replace the memories that are causing us the pain and hurt.

I am going to give a few examples—but remember only use these if you need to—don't jump right in and try these—you really need to be ready to use them...You need to have your thoughts in a fairly healthy place or these rituals will be nothing more than a dramatic exercise that has no lasting effect on your psyche.

So what do I mean by these rituals...allow me to explain: These rituals are acts that etch a lasting memory or visual – a memory or visual so powerful that you can draw on it again and again for strength when you need it. If I can share a story with you that will illustrate what I mean...

Several years ago I had a dog named Marius...Marius was a great dog that loved to swim in the kiddie pool that I purchased for him... only one day I filled the water up a bit too high and he drowned when he jumped in—and I was too late to save him....I loved that dog but felt helplessly responsible for his death and carried the guilt and shame around with me for over a solid month—I'm talking depression, as evidenced by an inability to sleep, eat, participate in activities that I normally enjoyed—I was able to continue working---but life was just tough....I knew rationally that I had loved that dog like no one else could have—but that I had made a mistake, and that my mistake contributed to his death...I knew that continuing on in the unhealthy way that I had been doing (continuous blaming myself, negative, self loathing, guilt and shame) was only going to cause further depression—so I conducted a ritual activity to assist me with the pain, guilt, and helplessness I was feeling after the death of Marius...

It took a long time for me to be ready to implement this ritual— many weeks of soul searching and efforts to replace negative thoughts with neutral or positive ones—many efforts involving talking with friends and supports--but when all else failed I turned to a ritual to help relieve the burden of my own thoughts and pain. I was totally committed and ready to allow the ritual to work—and that is where you need to be when using a ritual...

So, once I recognized that I was ready to apply a ritual to assist me in burning new thoughts and memories to replace old painful thoughts and memories, I took a few helium balloons and a permanent marker and I wrote all of the negative emotions that I had been carrying around with me onto the balloons....every negative emotion that I was feeling—every one that I could think of was written onto these balloons until they were practically covered with ink…

So, these balloons had "Guilt" and "Shame" and "Pain" and "Hurt" and "Self Loathing" among other descriptive words written on them until they were covered……….All of the negativity that I had carried around for the month following Marius' death was illustrated on those few balloons…

Holding the strings of the balloons, I engaged myself in deep thought over what I was about to do—and I committed to the following: When I let go of these balloons I am letting go of all of the negative feelings inside of me that have been dragging me down…I am letting go of these thoughts forever—I am letting go of the power that these thoughts have over me and setting myself free of them…..I am setting myself free of the guilt, shame, blame and depressing thoughts that had been ruling my existence for the last month—and committing to that letting go….

This did not mean that I loved Marius any less—**it just meant that I loved myself enough not to let these emotions destroy my life**, as they had been doing…

I released the balloons and watched them fly towards the clouds…further and further they traveled with the wind…I made myself watch the balloons fly – further and further away for several minutes until even with squinting, I could not see them anymore.

As the balloons got farther out of sight and left my field of vision, so did my negative feelings begin to leave my being— the balloons flying away symbolized my negative emotions flying further and further away from my consciousness….This didn't mean that I never had guilt or pain again—it just meant that when I did feel the occasional negative feelings connected to Marius' death I could reflect back on the balloons floating out of sight and the symbols they represented (my negative feelings) and let those feelings go all over again….I could immediately draw strength from the visual memory of the balloons flying further out of sight and drew a connection to the feelings they represented and it was a lot easier to let the feelings go – just as I had let the balloons go….

I had used a ritual to create and burn into my brain a new, lasting memory to ease the pain and hurt of a negative memory---and that is what you can do with the hurt and pain from your relationship break up.

The balloon idea works very well, or if you're safe with fire you can write your negative feelings down on paper and when you're ready to leg go of them you can set them ablaze……….bottom line is whatever you do you need to be committed to the idea that when the vehicle of your ritual is gone so are the negative feelings—this can be difficult – but you can do it! Be **thorough,** be **committed** and be **ready**---don't jump into the ritual if you are not all three! Otherwise it will just be empty and not effective. If done correctly, it can be one of the most effective tools in dealing with negative memories…

Other ideas for rituals is writing down all of your feelings on paper and tearing them up or sending them through the shredder… Choose a ritual that will work for you the best—and then, if you're ready, go for it……Good luck and happy ritual!

CHAPTER NINE

"Am I Ready?"

The question of "Am I ready?" refers to are you ready to get back out there and date again....well only you are capable of answering that question---but I am capable of asking you questions that will help you explore your readiness...Just what you needed me for, right? C'mon, I am here to help!

Let's say that you have been able to implement all of the principles in this book so far—and you are making progress...does that mean that you are ready?

I will be the first person to admit that there is no better way to forget that person that caused you heartache than by finding someone new...this is a proven technique that spans the ages...but are you ready to make the next relationship a better one that doesn't once again end in pain and hurt feelings? I know that this is what you wish for and want—but that doesn't mean that just because you wish for it and want it that it will happen...and if you rush into a new relationship before you are ready you may be setting yourself up for another round of relationship meltdown and subsequent heartache...

So make sure that you are ready before engaging in another love. You owe it to yourself and the person that you may now be interested in...Here are a few tips to see if you are ready:

1. When you think of your ex, are your thoughts hostile, negative, hurtful or disrespectful? Or are you putting your mantra to good use? If you're putting your mantra to good use then that is a good sign that you are ready. If you've gotten beyond the need for using your mantra, then it an excellent sign that you are ready!

2. If you hear your ex's name mentioned, what is your first gut initial reaction? Is it to feel hurt and pain, or is it indifferent or neutral? If it is hurt or pain then you are most likely not ready to begin a new relationship---but if it is indifferent or neutral, then perhaps you have defused and decreased the bondage the hurt has had over you and you are ready...

3. How do you feel about yourself? Are you doing for others? Do you have a healthy sense of worth and self esteem? If you don't yet, keep practicing the principles in this book—if you don't give it some more time because you don't want to enter into a new relationship in an unhealthy state of mind—that can spell disaster and will result in unhealthy outcomes—and haven't we had enough of those already?

4. Can you carry on a conversation and speak of your ex in positive terms? If not, then you may still be carrying around bitterness or resentment over the break up and that is not a good sign in moving forward in a new relationship...do you think your new partner wants to hear you badmouthing your ex? Most likely they won't stick around for fear that you will badmouth them at some point too...

5. Can you allow yourself to have a good time? Many people after a break up just seem to not be able to enjoy themselves...Can you let loose and be yourself? If so

that is a good sign that you are ready—and that you are not shackled by the weight of the thoughts of the hurt and pain—and instead you are buoyed by the thoughts of the opportunities that lie ahead.

There are many more questions that you may want to ask yourself—but the main ones are listed---such as "What are my motivations for wanting to be with another person—is it because I want to get back at my ex?" This is not a good reason for being with someone else—so weigh the answer to this question heavily...and what of the thoughts of wanting to be with another just to make ourselves feel wanted, attractive and desirable? Human nature will play this one out for many of us—but again—are you really in a healthy place to be with someone else if this is your motivation? And is this motivation fair to the other 'new' person that you are thinking of getting involved with?

Just remember that rushing into anything is risky and is your heart healthy enough for risky business? Can your fragile heart take another hit? Are you being fair to the person you are pursuing if your main intention is to use them to forget the ex?

Be honest with yourself—and the answer to the question "Am I ready?" will come...and then be honest with your answer and follow it with the same conviction that you are following the principles in this book...If you do this you cannot go wrong. Nice job!

Chapter ten

"Let's review"

Remember me asking you to keep an open mind and to apply the principles in this book? Well that is how I will start the review— these two things are paramount to being successful and to using the tools in this book to help you. If you can do these two things successfully, you are on your way!

It's ok to let yourself cry if you feel the need to...crying helps us get out unhealthy emotions from our souls—and frees us to feel again...it is an expression that needs no words-powerful in its ability to cleanse and purge our beings from the toxins that are negative feelings, memories and emotions.

Give things a little time. I will spare you all of the "Rome wasn't built in a day" quotes – and just say this: you didn't fall in love overnight (probably) so it makes sense that you won't recover overnight...sometimes time is just the best healer—but that doesn't mean that you cannot help along the process some by following the principles in this book...

Learn to express yourself and learn to do it often – especially immediately after the break up...of course we want to express

ourselves appropriately—but the main point here is to get the feelings associated with the break up out of your being and allow room for positive feelings to come into our being...holding onto negative emotions is not healthy and it may hold us back from moving forward in the healing process. So, arrange a venting session with a friend, or pick up that guitar and play, or journal your feelings in a notebook, or crank up the tunes in the car and sing along loudly, or write that poem that will make everyone cry, or paint a picture---you get the idea---pick a medium and use it to express your feelings—this is very therapeutic...bad feelings out makes room for good feelings in!

What's the fastest way to feeling better about ourselves? By doing something for others! That's right—when you are feeling down or worthless, the fastest way to restoring our feelings of self worth and self-esteem is by doing something for someone else. Chances are that your feelings of self worth and self esteem took a hit when the break up occurred---to help in regaining those feelings, try doing something nice for someone else...it will take your mind off of yourself and the troubles you are experiencing, it will help someone else in need, and it will give you a sense of purpose and meaning that you probably are missing...it is a win/win/win situation....so just do it! You will immediately start feeling better, and you will be focusing on others instead of yourself—which is what you need after a break up!

Create a mantra that you can repeat to yourself especially when you want or are tempted to say or think negative things about your ex. Thinking negatively about your ex is normal after a break up—the problem with this is that it can become a habit and detrimentally impact how we end up feeling about ourselves...Do we want to think of ourselves as the person that always is thinking negatively? Chances are that will make us feel like a negative person and translate into us not liking ourselves much...So, instead of being a "Negative Nancy", create a mantra that reflects positively on your ex and recite it to yourself every time you feel like going the negative route. This will make yourself feel better in the long run because you have consciously chosen to take the "High Road" and avoided being the negative person that you know that you don't want to be! This approach will also assist us in focusing on the good memories of the relationship and discourage us from dwelling on the painful memories and the hurt that came with the ending of it...

Hand over your concerns that you cannot control to your Higher Power—and trust that He/ She/ They will take care of them for you...You cannot control everything—and it can be very comforting to know that your Higher Power will take care of your worries that are outside of your control. If you consistently try to control things that you cannot you will increase your anxiety and stress, and your health (physical and mental) may suffer. So, utilize your Higher Power to its fullest and focus your efforts onto the things which you can control.

Were you the perfect 'significant other' during the relationship that just ended? Probably not if we are to be perfectly honest... so look inside of yourself and do an inventory of how you could have been a better boyfriend or girlfriend...chances are you will find several ways in which you could have been a better mate---if you really want to improve the next relationship you get into, work on these areas that beg for self-improvement and become a better 'you'...in the long run a little self inventory and efforts towards improving yourself now will result in an improved self esteem, an improved sense of responsibility, an increased sense of self-determinism and leave you better prepared to enter your next relationship. This may ultimately result in a more successful relationship outcome—and isn't that what we all are striving for?

Seek out your friends—they can help you through this tough time...talk to them, do things with them, allow them to help you by listening and providing companionship...Your friends are your lifeline and will help keep you grounded during this time of need. Don't think that you are being a bother to them by using them for support—you would do the same for them if and when they needed it, right? That is what friends do for one another and now it's your turn to be on the receiving end.

Use rituals to create and burn new memories into your brain to replace old, painful, hurtful ones...rituals can be very effective in helping us to erase negative tapes that play in our heads...the sounds, the thoughts and the pictures that we find so hard to forget...it may be the words that your ex spoke on the night you broke up or the visual of your ex with someone else that plays in your mind...these memories make it very difficult to think about anything else—and sometimes applying a ritual can be very helpful in replacing these memories with a new, powerful one so that you can continue your progress forward...Don't jump to using rituals too soon—you must be fully committed and ready—but when you do use one it can be extremely effective!

You feel as though you are in a better place and you wonder if you're ready for a date or to be with someone else—or perhaps you just want to be with someone else to try to get yourself into a better place...be careful here because sometimes the best intentions lead to worse feelings of despair and worthlessness... In order to begin a healthy relationship, we need to be in a healthy place ourselves. Be sure to ask yourself the important questions before you take steps to be with someone else...otherwise you may just be setting yourself up for more hurt and pain—and haven't we suffered enough of that already!???

CHAPTER ELEVEN

"Pep Talk"

Surviving a break up is and can be a devastating thing to live through…chances are at some point in life it will happen to you—that is the nature of relationships…Whenever you are dealing with something as unpredictable as another person and their emotions, you can never tell what might happen.

The key is keeping yourself in tact as much as possible before, during and after the break up. This book is designed to assist you with surviving the break up and thriving through the break up and beyond.

There will undoubtedly be times after the break up in which you may want to give up or that you may think that the principles are not working. HANG IN THERE! This is normal—not every day is going to be easy—but I want you to know that you are not alone…Many others have walked in your shoes—and many others have found that by applying the principles in this book that they can alleviate much of the pain and hurt by keeping an open mind, applying the principles and by emailing me if you need additional support…Peteangmgtman@aol.com.

Remember that this book is not meant as a replacement for therapy or psychiatric care—and that I wholeheartedly recommend professional help if your break up has contributed to feelings of helplessness, hopelessness, depression or suicidal or homicidal ideology. This is important and cannot be stressed enough—take care of yourself in whatever ways necessary so that you can be engaged in another relationship – one that is healthy, uplifting and rewarding…You deserve it! You can achieve it!

If this book has helped you in any way, drop me a line and let me know…if you think it can be helpful to someone you know that is suffering through a relationship break up, be a good friend and lend it out to them or let them know where they can get a copy.

Most relationships don't last and that is what makes engaging in one difficult-there is risk involved…the dissolution of a relationship doesn't have to be a devastating experience in which we lose a large portion of our lives for an extended period of time—suffering with the negative emotions that ensue--and this book intends to assist us in making surviving a relationship break up without the loss of time, energy and spirit, a reality. Together we can get through this, survive to love another day, and to increase our sense of self worth along the journey—so that ultimately we are someone that likes ourselves more, someone that has the capacity to love more, and someone that can enjoy what we all are striving for: A healthy relationship that fulfills all of our wants and needs…

Good luck in your individual journey---I will be walking along with you through the words in this book!

A bit about the author, Pete Taylor:

Pete Taylor is a licensed, clinical, professional counselor that is nationally certified (USA) and licensed to practice counseling in the state of Maryland. He earned his Bachelors Degree and Masters Degree from Towson University in Towson, Maryland.

Pete has always had an interest in working with people, and a specific interest in the dynamics of people in and out of relationships. He conducted healthy relationships groups in the detention centers of Baltimore County, Maryland while working as a therapist in 2002 and '03, and has performed couples counseling as well as individual counseling as part of a private practice that he has operated since 2004.

Although his specialty remains anger management and domestic violence counseling, he has a special place in his heart for those affected by the pain and suffering of broken relationships, and this book is a direct reflection of that special place in his heart.

Pete currently resides in Baltimore, Maryland and works as the director of a community based program that assists people in need. He enjoys writing self-help books with the intention of helping others improve their lives through the sharing of psychological principles and opinions learned and formulated through his educational and social experiences...

He hopes that you find some assistance in the pages and words of this book, as it has been therapeutic for him to write it for you. Pete encourages anyone that has questions or comments to email him at the below address.

Email: Peteangmgtman@aol.com

Thanks for purchasing this book. It is my sincere hope that it has assisted you in some way, and that in some way your life is better through reading it. Remember to take care of yourself and best wishes!

Absolutely, Positively, the Easiest Anger Management Book You'll Ever Need

By: Pete Taylor M.A., LCPC

Trafford rev. 09/27/2011

Trafford
PUBLISHING®   www.trafford.com

North America & international
toll-free: 1 888 232 4444 (USA & Canada)
phone: 250 383 6864 ♦ fax: 812 355 4082

For the love of my life and my reason for living…Bryanna, your smile, sense of humor and zest for life is a wondrous thing…I absolutely, positively LOVE being your Daddy. ☺

Hello, and thanks for picking up this book. I promise you that if you are looking for help with managing your anger, this book is absolutely, positively the easiest book you could have chosen to help you. That doesn't mean to imply that managing anger is easy. If it was, you wouldn't need any help, and you wouldn't be reading this right now. Managing anger can be one of the toughest struggles a person may go through in their life, and one of the most painful and costly. This book is not designed to bore you with statistics or stories, it is designed to help you in a straightforward, no-nonsense way. So, if you are looking for a book with a nice soft edge to its' text, this is not it. In the next few pages I am going to give it to you straight, and ask you to level with yourself. I'm not selling any cures for anger, so be forewarned: it's going to take some work on your part. I know that you are motivated because you're still reading, so let's get to it.

You may have already noticed that this is not a hulking, thick book with lots of charts and tables, or fancy exercises that you have to do each day. This is not an accident! I have seen those types of books—you've probably seen them too. You know the ones that have the book that explains all about your anger, and then maybe another one that has a million exercises for you to do to help you discover the causes of anger, the triggers for your anger, the types of anger, the consequences of your anger, what middle name you give your anger, what color your anger is and so on and so on forever!!

I certainly have seen these books, and even tried a couple of them. That is why I wrote *this* book! The other books were so thick and cumbersome that I felt defeated before I ever got started. Yes, I freely admit that I, at one time, had difficulty managing my anger. Those books collected dust on my corner tables, they never helped me, girlfriends left me, and family members steered clear of me, all because of my anger. I know the last thing you want to hear is my sob story of how I used to be a raging bull and all of the misery anger caused me…and how now I am a teddy bear that manages his anger a million times better than I used to, so I will spare you the boring

details. You are reading so that you can improve your own lives, not be put to sleep by the details of mine! Let me just say that I realized that I had a problem and went looking for a solution.

My search took me to bookshops, counselors, social workers, friends—heck, I even asked strangers for their opinion when I thought I might learn something! I had the desire to change, and that is important, but knowing **how** to change is important too! This book hopes to give you the insight you need on how to change. It can be done. I am living proof. I say that this book "hopes" to give you the insight you need to change, and if it does, to you this book could seem to be the greatest thing since sliced bread. But, if you don't have an open mind to accept the principles, or the motivation to put them into motion, you're just going to be the smartest angry person around and you will not have been helped at all!

Now I can't tell you my whole life story, and frankly, you probably don't want to hear it, unless you've got insomnia. But I feel the need to give you at least the Reader's Digest condensed version of my background. Here goes, don't blink or you'll miss it: As a counselor (Master's Degree from Towson University; Towson, Maryland), I have worked with some of the angriest people, and I have seen them make changes in their lives through the principles discussed in this book. I have counseled perpetrators of domestic violence, inmates in detention centers (men and women), individuals and couples experiencing divorce, teenagers (no further description needed!), sexual abuse victims, people who have been fired from their jobs, substance abusers, domestic violence survivors, wounded warriors returned home from combat and more…I have worked with individuals, couples, groups, families, step families of all ages, shapes, colors and sizes…What do all of these people have in common? They all had experienced anger and it affected their lives in negative ways. Not all of these people wanted help. Some of these folks were forced by the courts into working on their anger problems. Not all of these people improved, but all of them gained a better understanding of

what was driving their anger. This smidgeon of understanding is what I call insight or awareness.

It wasn't until I spoke with a very wise friend of mine that I uncovered a tiny clue to helping me with my own anger demons. It was through talking with him that I gained my smidgeon of insight. This friend clued me in on where my anger was coming from. I had to take his clue and do some investigative research on my own to find some answers, but I found them. You can too after getting your clues from this book.

I would give you my friend's name and phone number but I don't think he would appreciate all the calls he would get, and if you talk to him, you wouldn't need to read the book! I am kidding of course. But I am not kidding about the lesson here: Humor can be helpful, and I love a good laugh. I hope you bring with you an open mind and a sense of humor as you read through this book. An open mind is totally necessary, while the sense of humor is optional. Remember though, both can go a long way in helping you manage your anger.

Think of your brain as being a huge filing cabinet with all of the information that you have ever learned stored in it. You have a folder in that filing cabinet marked 'anger management' – and in instances in which you need to manage your anger your brain goes to that folder for suggestions on what to do…Everyone has one of these folders. But what does your folder have in it? Does your folder suggest yelling or screaming? Destroying property? Hurting people? Isolating yourself or sulking? Some people's folders have great strategies for managing their anger that produce great results---chances are you folder doesn't because you are reading this book… This book is designed to give you some more tools or 'suggestions' to put into your folder so that the next time you are in a situation in which you need to manage your anger you will have more options---healthier options---options for managing your anger that will help

you to feel better about yourself--- options that will increase and improve the quality of your life.

The bottom line is this: If I can help some of the angriest people I know (and I was one of those people), then I believe that I can help you. You are already on your way to a better way of life, because you have shown the motivation to read this far, and this tells me that you do have a desire to manage your anger. Remember, a desire to want to change is the first step. Now as we take our second and third and fourth steps, try to keep up. This book is designed to be an easy read. We don't want to bog you down in heavy chapters, we want you to be able to get the goods and start putting them into practice!...So let's go. Good luck, and don't forget I will be right here with you the whole way, you have my word. You can also email me for support if you need to at Peteangmgtman@aol.com...how many authors will offer that?

CHAPTER ONE:

<u>Getting Started</u>

You bought the book, right? You're started!! C'mon, times-a-wasting! (I told you that the chapters were easy to read!—here's where the sense of humor comes in handy!)

CHAPTER TWO:

<u>Anger</u>

I'm no dictionary, so I am going to give you a straightforward definition of anger that you can remember. Why? Because you need to know what anger is, not just the agony it causes. Some army general once said, "Know your enemy"...I have no idea who that was, and he's probably dead now, but it seems fitting. Here goes:

Anger is a normal emotion. Simple enough definition?

Oh yeah, and it is usually accompanied by hostility. The 'hostile feelings' part you probably already know. You have probably experienced them more than you care to remember. The normal emotion part is the part I want you to remember. It is normal to get angry. What is not normal is how some people act when they are angry. You know what I mean: the yelling, destruction of property, saying hurtful things about people, slamming doors, sulking, physical aggressiveness—the list could go on and on...did you hear anything in that list that sounded like you? Keep reading...

You've been angry a million times before you ever picked up this book and you will be angry a million more times after you have read

this book. **It is normal to get angry**, because **everyone gets angry**. Please don't forget that.

You are not some kind of freak because you get angry. If you *never* got angry you *would* be a freak. If anybody ever tells you that they never get angry, you have them call me and *I* will call them a freak! In fact I will call them a freak and a liar, because it is impossible to never get angry. It is possible to be able to manage your anger the majority of the time. Can you manage your anger 100% of the time? That is tough, we are only human. Even I get angry, and I wrote this book! It is normal. Can I remind you one more time that anger is normal? OK, thanks.

With all of that said, on to chapter three! Hang with me—this book is designed to get to the point *and* be an easy read.

CHAPTER THREE:

<u>Where does anger come from?</u>

I am going to spare you the misery of digging up your past, and reliving your childhood to uncover skeletons in your closet that may contribute to your difficulties with managing your anger. This is the 'absolutely, positively easiest anger management book you'll ever need' remember? If we were to dig up all of that old stuff you would need a therapist and a couple of years to sort through it. We are not going there—but I will say that if you think you can benefit from seeing a counselor, I recommend it, seriously. I am a licensed counselor and therapy can be extremely helpful – so it may be something to consider…

So, instead of pulling a Sigmund Freud and asking you how your mother or father treated you when you were little, I am going to assume the following: there are times when you get angry, and your anger causes you problems, and all of this is happening in the present time, and you may not even be interested in whether your childhood experiences are playing a part in all of this or not, right? You want some help with the here and now—some relief from what is causing problems for you now, right? OK, we're on the same page.

You just want to understand your anger now, where it is coming from and what to do about it. I can't blame you. You are no-nonsense! My kind of reader! So let's take a look at where anger comes from.

Anger comes from two places: **Things we do to ourselves**, and **things that happen to us**. Knowing the difference, and being able to distinguish between these two origins of anger is helpful.

Let's take the first origin: **What we do to ourselves**

We do some things to ourselves that make us angry, but the main thing that we are guilty of that causes us anger is **how we talk to ourselves**. Did you ever listen to the thoughts you tell yourself? Can you believe how we let ourselves talk to ourselves?!! OK, before I lose you, we all talk to ourselves. Our **self-talk** is that inner voice we all have that communicates our thoughts to us. If you have more than one inner voice, and they are telling you to do bad things, stop reading this book and call 911! I am kidding, for now just tell those extra voices to pipe down and let you continue reading.

Self-talk is that little voice inside our heads that is constantly with us. It is that voice you hear the first thing in the morning when you are staring at your mug in the mirror that says "Wow, you look great tiger!" or "You really over did it last night" or "That diet is really working" or "I need to drop ten pounds" – You get the picture, I'm sure.

Well, this voice can also sound like this: "That son of a -----, just cut me off, I'll show him!" or "She did that on purpose just to make me mad!" or "Everyone is against me!" or "I can never do anything right!". Whatever the self-talk, it can be powerful!

Consider this: Our thoughts influence how we feel. Agreed? Also, our feelings influence how we act. This is worth repeating: **Our thoughts influence how we feel, and our feelings influence**

how we act. See how our thoughts eventually impact our behaviors? With anger it is the same way. Think angry thoughts and you will feel angry. Feel angry and you will act angry.

Did you ever have a day in which you just felt so good—you know the type of day: You are looking great in your favorite shirt or blouse, you're experiencing the one great hair day for the month, the first person you ran into told you that you looked fabulous, you hit every green light on the way to the store—and you were thinking to yourself that you were pretty special, right? (If you don't have too many of these days that's ok, but it's good to have these types of days every once in a while!)

Well there you are, thinking that you're special, and how did this make you feel? Pretty darn special, am I right? Sure! And how did feeling special make you act? Carefree, happy, on top of the world, probably. And it all started with one thought: "Wow I really look good in this shirt!"

Now let's look at the other side of the coin to illustrate how mighty our self-talk can be. How do you suppose the person feels whose self-talk sounds like this: "I'm worthless, no good and unlovable"?

Chances are that if you're thinking, "I'm worthless, no good and unlovable", you're going to be feeling sad, depressed, worthless, and down. How does the person who is feeling sad, depressed, worthless and down act? They may cry, mope around, isolate themselves, stay in bed all day, or even kill themselves. That is right, they may even kill themselves. And it all started out with a single thought: "I'm worthless". See how powerful our self-talk is!!

So what does all of this mean? It means that **we have to check our self-talk**. It is the one thing we can control that contributes to us getting angry! If your self-talk is angry, chances are you are angry.

Remember how thoughts influence feelings, and feelings influence actions? Self-talk is at work inside of your head right now.

Here's some specific things to check or to 'listen' for in regards to your self-talk:

1. **How do you perceive situations, comments, or events?**
   Do you interpret things in an angry way? If your perceptions are angry, chances are your self-talk is angry, which means chances are, *you* are angry.

   Here's an example of how a perception can make you angry:

   Imagine Tom and Sally are walking down a crowded city sidewalk and a man walking towards them attempts to squeeze between the two and as he's squeezing, his shoulder happens to bump Sally.

   Sally's Perception: "The sidewalk was crowded and he was trying his best not to bump either one of us, but he did, it was just a harmless accident".

   Tom's Perception: "That jerk bumped you on purpose because he doesn't care about anyone but himself!" or "I think he's trying to start a fight by bumping you".

   You see how our happy couple experienced the same situation, but each one perceived it in a different way? Sally's version allows her to go on her merry way while Tom's version has him ready to fight. How do you choose to perceive the situations in your life?

2. **What do you hope for or expect from yourself and others around you?** Chances are if your expectations are set really high, you are being let down a lot and disappointed a lot.

This could be a source of anger too. If we try to keep our expectations as realistic as possible, it may cut down on disappointment, and cut down on anger quite significantly! I like to say that hopes come in three flavors: What we hope for from ourselves, what we hope for out of others and what we hope for from situations...in any case, keep all of your hopes and expectations realistic and you will save yourself much disappointment. As we will discover later, disappointment can easily be MASKED by anger!

Bottom line? **We control our self-talk,** so if it is making us angry, we can change it. Here's how (but it isn't easy, believe me and it takes practice!):

Remember the three R's:
1. <u>Realize</u> the negative, angry self-talk is present and challenge it!
2. <u>Replace</u> the negative, angry self-talk with positive thoughts, and
3. <u>Reinforce</u> your efforts by giving yourself a pat on the back for trying, and telling yourself good things about you like "I'm trying, and that's a start!"

Self-talk is what we do to ourselves that can make us angry, and I beat the idea that we are in control of our self-talk to death because I want you to know that when it comes to self-talk, **we have the power to control it!** It is not easy – but we have the power!

Now how about those things that happen to us from outside forces??

These are the things that happen to us that make us angry. You know, like the weather, or the person driving two miles an hour in front of us when we're late for work, or the judge that gives you a heavy fine for speeding but lets the cute blonde off with a warning, or the parent that beat you when you were little, or the person that

honks their horn outside of your house at three in the morning, or… OK, you get the point, we cannot control these things. **We can, and need to control how we react to these things** and that is what I want you to remember. **We are ultimately responsible for what we do!** No excuses!

When things happen to us that we cannot control, and we get angry as a result, ask yourself, "Is this something I can control?". If the answer is 'no', then go to work with your self-talk. If your self-talk is angry as well, then the part that you are in control of (the self-talk) is not helping the problem, it is hurting you. (See the three "R's").

If something happens to you, like the guy in back of you bumps you while you are waiting in line at the grocery store, and you start having angry thoughts to yourself about how he did it on purpose (remember perceptions!) or how inconsiderate a boob he must be, this is angry negative self-talk at work making the situation even worse! Chances are your self-talk is making you more upset! Changing angry or negative self-talk takes practice—remember you spent how many years developing your habits of self-talk? More than you care to admit probably, and it is going to take more than reading a few chapters and trying the three R's a few times to have it change. HANG IN THERE! KEEP PRACTICING!! This is just a start. IT TAKES SOME TIME!!

My hope is that now **you may be more aware of your self-talk** and **how it may be affecting your ability to manage your anger.** Another hope of mine is that you might really try the three R's!

I had to mention self-talk first because it is so important. When you put this book down, your self-talk will be there, when you eat dinner tonight, your self-talk will be there, when you wake up

tomorrow, your self-talk will be there. I want you to become more aware of it, that's all. **Is it helping you, or hurting you?**

One last thought on self-talk (if you can take one last thought on self talk!): Someone once mentioned to me that self-talk is like taking someone with you wherever you go. If you are constantly self-talking in a negative or angry way, you have chosen to take with you a person that is going to bring you down...maybe even an enemy. If you're self-talk is positive and constructive, you have chosen to take with you a person that is a helping you or someone that is a calming influence...maybe like a best friend. **Who do you choose to take with you everywhere you go?**

Stick with me, chapter four is next, and I promise, if you look for some clues to your anger, you will find them in chapter four!

Chapter Four:

What's behind the MASK?

We all wear masks from time to time…Halloween, costume parties, that fake face you make when your mother-in-law asks you what you think of her lasagna (just kidding!)…But did you know that when we are angry we are wearing a mask too? Yup. We are. I call it the angry MASK.

If there is one concept in this book that may be the hardest to grasp, it is this idea about wearing an angry MASK. I am giving you 'heads up' on this because I want you to know up front that this is not an easy concept to swallow, especially for guys. WHY? Because **it requires us to get in touch with our feelings and emotions.** A lot of you out there are now reacting as if I wrote a bunch of dirty words—*feelings? emotions? getting in touch with them?* Now before you throw the book down like it was covered in leaches, never to pick it up again, give me a chance to explain, and then make up your own mind as to whether you think this mask thing makes sense or not, OK? I have been up front with you so far, and I'll keep telling you like it is if you give me the chance. Thanks, I'm glad you're willing to keep that open mind, really.

OK, originally, when devising my strategy for managing anger, M-A-S-K was an acronym for **My Anger Starts Kit**. Cute, right? I did this because I wanted you to be aware of where your anger originates or starts…If it helps you remember the idea about the mask, great… if you forget the acronym two minutes after you put down the book that is fine too, it's not that important! What is important is that you understand the principle of the angry MASK.

The angry MASK in a nutshell is this: **Anger is a secondary emotion**. What does this mean? It means that as far as your feelings are concerned, anger comes second, after some other emotion. I know what you're thinking: "C'mon, when I get angry, I just get angry. There aren't any other emotions hanging around!" It's all right to think that way, for now…I'm hoping that after you read on, you may begin to start changing the way you think about your anger—and the angry MASK may be part of that changed thinking!

How many folks out there know someone that had his feelings hurt and as a result they got angry? How many folks out there know someone that suffered the disappointment of losing a job, or had a friend or lover tell you that they didn't want to be your friend or lover anymore and they got angry over it? How many of you know someone that got angry because they were embarrassed by someone or something? How many of you may know someone who lost a loved one and at the funeral they seemed bitter with anger? Know anyone that is angry with jealousy? How many of you know someone that gets a little testy when they are feeling frustrated? People that are worried or anxious or people that may be seriously ill sometimes get a little short tempered as they are waiting for the doctor. Have you ever felt angry or seen someone that was angry over any of the situations above?

All of the examples above demonstrate how anger is a secondary emotion. It comes after another emotion has already set the table or gotten to you first. Anger can MASK an underlying emotion, (the emotion that comes to you first) in any given situation.

The underlying emotion is the feeling that comes first. This underlying emotion can cause us discomfort. (Remember when we talked about being disappointed by unmet hopes or expectations? How many times have we gotten angry because we were disappointed?) When we feel the discomfort caused by the underlying emotion, sometimes we MASK the underlying emotion with anger to escape the discomfort. Hurt, fear, disappointment are just a few examples of underlying emotions that get MASKED by anger.

Consider this:

I was co-facilitating a class on Anger Management in a detention center, spreading the word of the angry MASK to the inmates when my partner noticed that my zipper was down. I hadn't a clue that I had left the barn door open, so to speak, but my partner noticed it for sure and made sure that everybody else knew it too, because she announced it loudly to the entire group! There I was parading around for at least thirty minutes in front of 25 inmates with my fly open! You guessed it! I was pretty embarrassed. I had several options at that moment in time of how to react (one of which was to zip up, which I did promptly!). One choice I had was that I could have gotten angry, because I may have perceived my partner's outburst as being motivated by trying to make fun of me or being purposeful in nature to embarrass me…but that wouldn't have looked very responsible for the guy teaching the anger management course to blow his top…another choice at my disposal was that I could have dealt with my embarrassment in a direct fashion.

Let me re-cap this little bit of a scenario real quick for fear of losing you:

1. **Something has to happen to get the anger ball rolling** (in this case my partner tells the whole world that my fly is open)
2. **I feel an underlying emotion** (this emotion was **embarrassment**)

3. **Discomfort** sets in (True! It is not comfortable being embarrassed)
4. **I have a choice:**
   I can **deal directly** with the discomfort of being embarrassed, or **MASK the embarrassment with anger.**

Why would someone MASK their embarrassment with anger? Here's why. We are very practiced at getting, being, and/or staying angry. We know how to do it! We are very comfortable with slamming doors, cursing or yelling loudly, giving dirty looks, punching walls, getting even, saying hurtful things, pacing the floor, threatening, clenching our fists, grinding our teeth, grabbing and holding someone, pushing or shoving, destroying property etc, etc...

What we are not practiced at is dealing directly or effectively with the feeling of being embarrassed. We tend to do what we feel more comfortable doing...in other words, **if we don't know how to deal with our embarrassment, or we don't want to deal with our embarrassment, we may choose the 'easier' path, and that is to put the angry MASK on and get angry instead.**

The angry MASK covers the embarrassment, and allows us to 'escape' the discomfort that comes with it. This is what I mean by the primary emotion (embarrassment) getting covered up by anger.

Haven't you ever seen or witnessed someone getting embarrassed and as a result they get very angry? This was the angry MASK at work. Their underlying emotion was embarrassment, but they did not deal directly with the embarrassment—they put on the angry MASK instead.

Any emotion that we feel can be masked by anger if the situation is right...

That statement is worth repeating: **ANY emotion can be MASKED with anger!**

It is a choice for us to put on an angry MASK.

Getting in touch with, and identifying our underlying emotion will go a long way in helping us manage our anger. How? Because **if we can identify our underlying emotion and learn constructive ways to deal with them, we do not need to put on an angry MASK at all!** This sounds easy right?

The problem is that we are not as practiced at dealing directly with our underlying emotions as we are at dealing with anger. We are not as practiced at having our feelings hurt, or feeling sad, or being disappointed, or grieving, or being afraid, or frustrated, or disrespected, or feeling anxious and the list of emotions that we are not very practiced at dealing with could go on and on.

So what we often do is MASK these emotions that cause us discomfort with anger. Anger puts us right back into a comfort zone because we know how be angry, act angry and sound angry.... and in many cases, we are pretty darn good at it! And in many cases it has become a second nature to react to these underlying emotions in this way...

Our brains are actually wired to help our bodies avoid uncomfortable feelings, so when we put on an angry MASK, and we avoid the discomfort, our brain thinks it is doing us a favor. The brain creates a 'shortcut' to the angry MASK to try to help us......

Often it is the case where we experience something (like someone cutting us off on the road, or a person in front of us in the 'ten items or less' check-out line with twenty two items) and it's like a button inside of us gets 'pushed' and we just get angry...it's like we skip right over the underlying emotion and go right to the angry MASK! This is what I call your hot buttons...they get pushed and you go straight from "something happens" to the angry MASK in no time flat...

The MASK theory asks you to challenge these shortcuts and dig deep underneath the surface of your anger to find the emotion hiding behind the angry MASK.

Think about the last time you got angry...really dig deep inside yourself and be honest...was there another emotion that could have been there under the anger? Were your feelings hurt? Or were you disappointed? Were you afraid? This is the time that you are really required to be honest with yourself, and try to understand what emotion came just before you put the angry MASK on. It may have occurred so fast that you never even realized that there was another emotion at work! That is usually how the angry MASK works...but I bet afterward when you calmed down a bit you could see how your anger may have been the result of the underlying emotion, and that you MASKED it with anger instead of dealing directly with it.

The anger acts as a defense mechanism and allows us to avoid dealing with the uncomfortable, underlying emotion(s). The problem is that after the anger comes and goes, the underlying emotion is often still there, it's just that it was covered up and suppressed!

Let me give you a couple of examples because it is really important for you to understand what is at the root of your anger, my anger, everyone's anger (in a nutshell)—it is these underlying emotions that we choose not to deal with!!

Anger is secondary—and you need to be able to **identify the underlying emotion** so that **you can learn to effectively deal with it.** The better you are at **dealing with the underlying emotion, the less you will have to put on the angry MASK**, and the better your life will be. I promise. But it does take work, and practice... and before I get too carried away, here are some examples illustrating what I mean:

Jim had a girlfriend. Every once in a while Jim's girlfriend would approach him and say, "We need to have a serious talk". Now I am not sure about what types of relationships you've had in the past, or if you're involved in a relationship right now, but usually when your significant other says that you need to have a serious talk, that usually spells bad news.

So Jim's girlfriend says "We need to have a serious talk" and Jim flails his arms, gets red in the face and shouts "You are always wanting to have a serious talk---well I am sick of you wanting to do that, so forget it!! If you want to have a serious talk, go stand in front of the mirror and talk to yourself!! I am out of here!!" And he proceeds to walk out of the house and slam the door behind him.

Why did Jim get angry? Most folks would say that he got angry because his girlfriend wanted to have a serious talk. If you answered that way, you have put all of the blame on Jim's girlfriend, and let Jim off the hook! **Remember the MASK whenever you see anyone angry**, or **whenever you are angry**. When you see someone who is angry, ask yourself, "I wonder what they are really feeling underneath that anger" because that is where the clues lie. Ask yourself, **"What underlying emotion are they covering up with the angry MASK?"**

In Jim's case, he was **afraid** of what his girlfriend wanted to talk about…remember, when your significant other wants to 'have a serious talk' it may often spell bad news! So he was feeling **FEAR** over having this talk. Fear was his primary emotion. But Jim didn't know how to deal with this fear, so he put the angry MASK on instead. Jim covered up his underlying emotion (Fear) with the angry MASK. If Jim had an effective way of dealing with his fear he could have avoided putting on the angry MASK altogether. Until he learns how to deal with his fear, he will continue to put on the angry MASK, and his relationship will suffer…Does this sound familiar to any of you reading?

Now if you can ask yourself when you see someone else that is angry "I wonder what they must be feeling that is underneath their anger?" can you ask that same question of yourself when you are angry?...

Can you ask the next time you find yourself angry, "What underlying emotion am I covering up with this angry MASK?" **The two emotions most commonly MASKED with anger are HURT and FEAR....Look for these two culprits underneath your anger!!**

Identify the underlying emotion, and you are on your way to understanding your anger at its' root.

Let's break it down like we did before with a handy little flow chart that chronicles the birth of Jim's anger:

1. **Something happened**: (Jim's girlfriend said she wanted to have the talk)
2. Jim felt an **underlying emotion**: (Jim, if he could be really honest with himself, would know that the idea of having a 'serious talk' with his girlfriend scares him to death, because he is afraid that he is going to hear her say something that will mean bad news to their relationship. **The underlying emotion Jim is feeling is FEAR**
3. This fear causes Jim to feel plenty of **discomfort.**
4. Jim has a **choice** to make: **Deal with the underlying emotion** (fear), or **MASK his underlying emotion (fear) with anger.**
5. In this instance, Jim has chosen to put on the angry MASK to cover his fear because he is more comfortable at this point with being angry than he is with dealing with being afraid. He may not know how to deal with being afraid, or he may not even be able to identify that he is afraid...

Jim probably has re-played this scene with his girlfriend so often that his reactions to his girlfriend wanting to talk have become almost automatic, and it may be hard for him to know or admit that he is afraid. When he hears the words "We have to have a serious talk" his automatic pilot takes over and he blows a gasket. Jim's '**hot button**' for getting angry is his girlfriend stating that she wants to have a serious talk!

It is my hope that these examples will give you a clear explanation of the MASK at work. Can you take one more? OK, here goes:

Judy has two teenagers. Every night it seems Judy tells her kids to pick up after themselves, and every night it seems Judy is always the one putting things away or straightening up the mess in the house. Judy comes home one night after working all day, opens the front door of the house and walks into the living room. She sees two jackets thrown on the floor, two book bags draped on the couch, dirty snack dishes on the corner table, the TV is blaring with music videos, and remnants of her kids' science projects, that Judy has asked to be picked up for the last week, are still on the floor, the couch, the coffee table etc. Judy sees the mess and she gets steamed.

Judy thinks that she "just got angry". Did she 'just get angry?' Or was there an underlying emotion that came before Judy put on her angry MASK?

What was the event that triggered Judy's emotions?

Was Judy in control of this event or was she not in control, or was it a little of both?

What was the underlying emotion that Judy felt?

Finally, I wonder if Judy was able to deal with the underlying emotions directly, or whether she put on her angry MASK?

Let's recap:

The event (or as I like to put it-"What happened?"): Judy comes home and **sees her house a wreck.** This was not controllable by her. We can never completely control another person's behavior, even our own children! Judy could not totally control whether or not her kids would listen to her and clean up after themselves. Of course, there were probably some controllable forces at work here too, because Judy probably **hoped** and **expected** the house to be cleaned up, and when it wasn't, she was let down and disappointed. She may have even **perceived** the mess as being left there by her kids as an act of defiance or that they didn't care or respect her wishes. Judy probably engaged in some **angry self-talk** as well, and who could blame her!

The underlying emotion: Judy could have felt a few different underlying emotions before she MASKED them. Some possibilities could be: Disappointment, disrespect, hurt, frustration to name a few. All of these caused her some level of **discomfort.**

The choice: Judy can blow her stack by putting on the angry MASK, or she can choose to deal with whatever emotions she is feeling. It is hard to picture this as a choice because sometimes anger strikes lightening fast, and we aren't even really aware that there was an original underlying emotion. **Anger is a choice**, and **if you're angry you have chosen to put on the angry MASK instead of dealing with the underlying emotion.** That statement, that anger is a choice, can be tough to swallow. Don't worry if you can't swallow it now…give yourself some time. Your reactions are normal. Anger is normal…what we are striving to do is to help you accept that **if you can identify the underlying emotion that is at the root of your anger and learn to deal with it constructively, you can avoid putting the angry MASK on altogether!**

Judy put on the angry MASK because at that instant of walking into her house to find it a mess, she found getting angry an easier,

more natural or more comfortable choice than dealing with the underlying emotions of disappointment/disrespect/frustration that she felt. The angry MASK had some advantages here—it allowed her to temporarily escape the disappointment/disrespect/frustration she felt towards her children, and allowed her to express that anger immediately....temporary escape and expressing your feelings sound like pretty good things, right? They are, but in the long run, Judy's ability to grow and maintain a healthy relationship with her children and have them understand her needs to have the house straightened up will suffer the more she decides to put on the angry MASK...

The mask allows us to escape those uncomfortable feelings caused by the underlying emotion, provides us a temporary relief from those uncomfortable feelings derived from the underlying emotion, and provides an outlet for expression. BUT, in the long run, the angry MASK destroys relationships. That is worth repeating: **Putting on the angry MASK again and again destroys relationships.**

Perhaps Judy has been through this same scenario with her kids a thousand times and never dealt with her underlying emotions directly, and the donning of the angry MASK has become second nature, or habit. Whatever the case, the sooner Judy gets practiced at identifying the underlying emotion (disappointment/disrespect/frustration/hurt), and gets practiced at dealing directly with that underlying emotion(s), the sooner her life and her relationship with her kids will improve exponentially. We will discuss dealing with underlying emotions in a later chapter, but remember: **Identifying the underlying emotion is a critical step** in choosing not to put on the angry MASK—deal with the underlying emotion **directly** instead!

So we don't risk losing anyone, let's do a quick review of the main points covered so far:

1. Anger is normal.
2. When you are angry, ask yourself, "Is my anger being caused by something I am doing to myself?" (self-talk

that I can control), or by "Something that is happening *to* me?" (something I cannot control), or a little of both?"

3. Is your self-talk helping you or hurting you during these times?

4. What underlying emotion sits under your angry MASK? Can you identify it? Sometimes we have to dig hard beneath the surface to find it, and sometimes we cannot find it until we've already blew our stack and we've calmed down. The underlying emotion is worth finding, even after you've blown a gasket—so you are better prepared for the next time it comes around. We must identify the underlying emotion before we can deal with it.

5. Are you MASKING your underlying emotion with anger? Answering this takes being brutally honest with yourself, and it takes some practice. Be honest, and keep practicing, you can do it!

Sometimes we cannot recognize what underlying emotion came before we put on the angry mask until hours, days or even years later. The hope of this book is to help you become better at recognizing the underlying emotions that precede your anger. Being able to recognize them and identify them more quickly so that you can deal with them more quickly is the idea here. Eventually, you may be able to recognize the underlying emotion so quickly, that you don't reach for the angry mask hardly at all. Wouldn't that be sweet! That is where we want to be!

Chapter Five:

<u>Quick Response Strategies (QRS's)</u>

Since anger is normal, and therefore happens to everyone, it is important to have some strategies at our disposal for when it occurs. Remember that flow chart? I have placed it below to remind you again of the roots of everyone's anger—they lie in the simple flow chart:

1. **Something happens**
2. **We feel an underlying emotion**
3. **The underlying emotion causes us discomfort**
4. **We have a choice: Deal with the underlying emotion or MASK it with angry MASK**

Well now we want to add a "number 5" to that flow chart: If and when you are at the point of number 4 (Dealing with the underlying emotion or putting on an angry MASK) and you choose to put on an angry MASK, go directly to number 5 below...

5. Use a Quick Response Strategy (QRS for short—these letters are in the same order as they appear in the alphabet—so they are easy to remember!)

"What the heck is a Quick Response Strategy?" you may be asking yourself...I would be asking the same thing if I didn't know already...

A **quick response strategy** is something you can do to **help calm yourself down** a bit so that you don't act out in an angry state of mind and behave in a way that you might regret.

A quick response strategy 'buys' your brain a little time to 'amp down' or 'chill out' before you decide how to act.

A short list of quick response strategies are to follow, but remember, QRS's are not a 'cure' or a 'fix' for your anger—they are not designed to 'manage' your anger---that comes from dealing more effectively with the underlying emotion (and we will discuss dealing with the underlying emotion soon, I promise!!)...QRS's are important because we know that anger will hit us sooner or later– it does everyone—and having an immediate plan of action when we recognize that we've got the angry MASK firmly implanted over the underlying emotion is a good idea so that we can avoid punching the guy at the bar, or avoid saying that hurtful comment to our mother, or avoid smashing the television set or putting a hole in the wall...

So here's a short list that probably will look familiar to you if you've tried to manage anger in the past---**but remember what an QRS is for—to buy us some time so that we can get our thoughts together and act in a better state of mind...**

Some examples of Quick Response Strategies:

1. **Deep Breathing**: Take a deep breath through your nose to the count of five...hold that breath for the count of five...then exhale out of your mouth to the count of five...do this several times...oxygen to the brain relaxes us...

2. **Visualization**: Visualize yourself in a setting much more calm and peaceful, like a beach or a quiet get away…let yourself get lost in the thoughts and pictures in your mind.

3. **Counting to ten** (or a hundred or a thousand – whatever the need might be): Believe it or not this can help…it occupies the mind and hinders negative self talk from taking control too quickly.

4. **Prayer**: Like they say, "When all else fails…" Prayer is a way of usurping (always wanted to use that word in a book) self talk's power over you…sort of a preemptive strike on self talk…

5. **Take a walk or a time out**: Remove yourself from the hostile situation…this is the oldest one in the book next to count to ten…but by removing yourself you change the scenery for your mind and make it easier for calming self talk to take place…

6. **Write down your feelings**: this is an excellent way of expressing your thoughts, getting things off your chest, and taking time for corrective thoughts to be born in your self talk.

There are many forms of QRS's and my hope is that you practice and get efficient at implementing at least one of these ways for yourself…remember: **It's normal to put on the angry MASK now and again, but when you do, USE A STRATEGY!!!**

Here's why using a strategy is so critical…

When you get angry, **one of the first negative consequences that takes place is that you stop thinking clearly** or rationally… usually your thinking becomes more hostile or aggressive…. remember a few chapters back when we talked about how thoughts influence feelings and feelings influence actions? Well, hostile or aggressive thoughts may eventually lead to hostile or aggressive feelings, which then lead to hostile or aggressive actions—and that

is what we are trying to avoid!! Hostile, aggressive actions sometimes lead to getting arrested!!

So, if you stop thinking clearly when you get angry, and your thoughts take on a more aggressive nature, there is an increased chance that your actions will take on an aggressive nature too. What **we want the QRS to do is to give our brains a little time to begin to start thinking more clearly**...for our emotions to lessen in intensity, so that our thoughts become less hostile...

less hostile thoughts = less hostile feelings = less hostile actions...

Here's an easy way to think about our thinking, which leads to our feelings, which in turn leads to our actions:

When we get angry our **E**motional thoughts (our "E" thoughts) become very loud inside our heads, and sometimes they can drown out our **I**ntellectual thoughts (our "I" thoughts)...Our **emotional thoughts are the ones that are screaming** things like "Don't let them get away with that!" or "Hit him!" or "They did that on purpose, I'll show them" when we are angry.....

Our **Intellectual thoughts are the thoughts in our heads that are trying to be the level headed ones** – you know the ones that try to remind us of what the consequences of our actions might be if we act out on the aggressive thoughts?

Our **I**ntellectual thoughts sound like this inside our heads "Don't do that, we might get arrested" or "That is hurtful, and unkind" or "That is not the right thing to do" only these thoughts are like a whisper compared to our **E**motional thoughts...

When we get angry our emotional thoughts are so loud that we cannot hear our intellectual thoughts, and when we ignore our

intellectual thoughts and make decisions based on our louder, more aggressive emotional thoughts, bad things usually happen.

Using an QRS allows our Intellectual thoughts a chance to gain some volume…and for our emotional thoughts' volume to get turned down a notch…this is good for our decision making and our impulse control…remember what we said about QRS's "buying our brain some time to start thinking a bit more clearly"? This is what we're talking about here.

So, when you put the angry MASK on, and we all will from time to time, use a QRS! It may be the difference between making the right decision or making a terribly wrong one…and remember that our "E" thoughts and our "I" thoughts need to be about the same volume in our heads in order for there to be a fair debate on how we're going to choose to act…using a QRS will help our "E" thoughts shrink a bit, and our "I" thoughts grow a bit so that they can debate each other inside our heads—and help us make more appropriate decisions….using an QRS gives our "I" thoughts a fighting chance!

CHAPTER SIX:

Dealing with our underlying emotions

Ok, so I hope you're with me so far…maybe even you've had an opportunity or two to dissect your anger in situations and figure out what your underlying emotion was, and how you may have masked it with anger…it's good to dissect our anger whenever we get a chance in search of that underlying emotion…The more practice we get at it the better we become at identifying the feeling under our anger…If you put on the angry MASK recently, did you use a strategy to buy your brain a little time to cool down before acting?

If you were able to identify the underlying emotion underneath your angry MASK, did you make an attempt to deal with it? What happened?

Did you avoid putting on the MASK by dealing directly with your underlying emotion? Did you manage your anger as a result?

That is what we are hoping for…that you can deal with the underlying emotion and therefore avoid putting the angry MASK on at all…So, **how *do* we deal with the underlying emotion?**

First things first…**we have to be able to identify the underlying emotion before we can deal with it…**This is the part that you need to be open minded and honest with yourself…especially men---Men have been socialized all of their lives to distance themselves from their underlying emotions and as a result it can be difficult to identify them---I said difficult, not impossible!

Once the underlying emotion is identified, we need to communicate.…

Once the underlying emotion is identified, we need to communicate and <u>express our feelings.</u>

This sounds easy, but it can be tricky. It becomes tricky because anger gives us lots of energy, and it plants within us a desire to express ourselves. This energy and desire sometimes can come out in a hostile manner—and that is something that we're trying to avoid…So, **after identifying the underlying emotion, we need to be aware of *how* we are going to communicate and express our feelings. This may be a good time to employ a QRS!**

Remember this: It is **dealing directly with the underlying emotion through communicating and expressing our feelings that will allow us to avoid putting the angry MASK on**—so we want to do a good job of it!

How do we communicate and express our feelings? Well, if we look at communicating as if it were a task or a job such as building a house, what do we need to build a house? If you answered money, you are correct—but the answer I was looking for was "tools". To build a house you need tools like a hammer, level, concrete mixer etc.

To communicate and express our feelings effectively you need tools as well, only slightly different tools than if we were building a house…**to communicate well, the tools we need are WORDS.**

To communicate and express your feelings effectively, the types of words we need are words that describe our emotions---I call them "emotional words".

There is a list of emotional words to follow...read them over and you will probably tell yourself "I know all of these words!" That is a good thing, but can you remember them when you need them—when you are trying to express how you feel to someone, when those feelings are causing you some discomfort?

Get as familiar with the list and add some of your own to build up your emotional vocabulary---the more tools you have the better. The more tools you have, the better house you can build...the more emotional words you can grab and express at a split second's notice, the better communicator you will be—and **the better you are at expressing your feelings, the better you will be at avoiding putting on the angry MASK....**

Emotional words list:

Aggressive	Alienated	Angry	Anxious
Apathetic	Bashful	Bored	Cautious
Confident	Confused	Curious	Depressed
Determined	Disappointed	Discouraged	Disgusted
Embarrassed	Enthusiastic	Envious	Ecstatic
Excited	Exhausted	Fearful	Frightened
Frustrated	Guilty	Happy	Helpless
Hopeful	Hostile	Humiliated	Hurt
Hysterical	Innocent	Interested	Jealous
Lonely	Loved	Love-struck	Mischievous
Miserable	Negative	Optimistic	Pained
Paranoid	Peaceful	Proud	Puzzled
Regretful	Relieved	Sad	Satisfied
Shocked	Shy	Sorry	Stubborn
Sure	Surprised	Suspicious	Thoughtful
Undecided	Withdrawn		

Add your own words to the list and become familiar with the words and how they connect to your feelings...**We need to be able to communicate and express our feelings in order to deal with our underlying emotions or else our only other choice will be to put on the angry MASK**, and that is what we are trying to avoid.... we are trying to decrease our use of the angry MASK by becoming better at identifying the underlying emotion and expressing how we feel – this takes an emotional word vocabulary that has lots of words in it and lots and lots of practice!

So, we have a good working list of our emotional words—and these will be our 'tools' for communicating our feelings...this is a good start....

Let's revisit our buddy Jim from Chapter Four...remember his girlfriend would tell him that she wanted to have a serious talk, and he would blow a gasket...

1. Jim's trigger was his girlfriend saying that she wanted to have a serious talk—this is **"What happened?"** to get the anger ball rolling....
2. Jim felt **FEAR** because he was afraid that his girlfriend was going to say something bad to him, like she wanted to break up, or that she didn't like the way he was treating her...**This is Jim feeling the underlying emotion: FEAR**
3. This fear causes **Jim to feel discomfort**
4. **Jim has a CHOICE: Deal with the Fear or put on an Angry MASK**

Of course in our example, Jim doesn't use a Quick Response Strategy, and he flies off the handle because he

A) Cannot identify his underlying emotion
B) Does not know how to deal with his underlying emotion

C) Does not want to deal with his underlying emotion
Or
D) All of the above

It may be one, two, three, or all of the reasons above that stop Jim from dealing with his underlying emotion.

Let's examine a few ways that Jim could have dealt with his underlying emotion if he would've just communicated and expressed his underlying emotion to his girlfriend: Consider the exchange between Jim and his girlfriend goes a little differently than it did in Chapter Four…What if it went like this:

Girlfriend:	"Jim, we have to have a serious talk"
Jim:	"Every time you say that you want to have a serious talk, I'm afraid that you're going to say something bad".

This little exchange that took maybe five seconds to accomplish has opened the door to communication for Jim and his girlfriend… he has begun to deal with his fear by expressing it……. "I'm **afraid** you're going to say something bad" he says to her. He has made a choice to express and deal with his underlying emotion, and not to put on the angry MASK! Way to go Jim!!

He identified that he was afraid (FEAR) and that by dealing directly with this fear he can avoid putting on the angry MASK… He deals directly with this fear by expressing and communicating his feelings to his girlfriend…this begins a dialogue between the two of them that helps Jim avoid becoming angry. Jim has broken the cycle or pattern of continuously putting on the angry MASK whenever his girlfriend says that she wants to have a serious talk by simply expressing his feelings…
It sounds easy for Jim…but we know that it is not always that easy…

First he had to identify the underlying emotion (FEAR)…and then he had to muster up the courage to express it (I'm afraid you're going to say something bad") It is tough getting in touch with our underlying emotions—but we have to do it if we want to reduce the use of the angry MASK…

Another tip that may go a long way in communicating and expressing our underlying emotions effectively, and one that might help us to deal with our underlying emotion directly are "I" statements…

An "I" statement is a statement that begins with the words "I feel" and then proceeds to use descriptive words to describe the emotions…here's an easy way to use an "I" statement:

Just fill in the blanks:

I feel _____ when _____ happens.
     Emotional word(s)   Description of the "What happened?"

Using "I" statements take practice, but they are designed for several purposes…the first being they help you identify and express your underlying emotion….this is key, because if you cannot identify your underlying emotion, you cannot deal with it—and if you cannot deal with it you have no other choice but to put on the angry MASK—an "I" statement helps with the identification of the underlying emotion and the expression of the feeling!! ☺

Secondly, "I" statements tend to help direct us away from their evil counterpart "You" statements…"You" statements are those that we tend to use when we are angry---any of these sound familiar?

"**You** make me so angry when you make so much noise when I am trying to watch the game!"

"**You** are the reason that I yelled—if you hadn't made me so mad I never would have acted like that"

"**You** are at fault! I didn't do anything wrong!"

Notice a pattern with the above statements? They all start with the word "you", and they all make someone feel as though they are being attacked.

"You" statements make the target of the statement feel defensive because they feel like you are attacking them...when someone gets defensive they only care about defending themselves and will stop listening to what you're saying....defensive people are nearly impossible to reason with—you probably know this already from the times that you have become defensive in the past...

"I" statements take away that feeling of 'attack' because they all start out with the word "I"...People usually don't become defensive when you are talking about yourself...their guard will stay down long enough for you to express your feelings, and then dialogue can happen...dialogue is good, defensiveness is bad...expression is good (gets things off your chest and lets the other person know what you are feeling), communication is good because it leads to dealing with the underlying emotion which leads us to using the angry MASK less!

So now I have some questions for you to ponder:

- Can you be honest with yourself and own your feelings?
- Can you be honest with yourself and identify and label your underlying emotions?
- Can you be a brave enough person to express what your underlying emotions are, instead of always reaching for the angry MASK?
- Can you use a strategy (QRS) to help your "E" thoughts shrink a bit and allow your "I" thoughts a chance to debate what your actions might or should be?
- Can you consider what the origin of your anger is— something you did towards yourself (self-talk in the

form of hopes/expectations and/or perceptions,) or something that was done towards you (frustrations, abuse or unfairness etc.)?

- Can you examine your self-talk and is it a calming presence in your head or does it add fuel to the anger fire?
- Can you practice using the three R's if your self-talk is negative?
- Can you make the effort to learn from the times in which you've chosen to put on the angry MASK by dissecting your anger?—to figure out what the underlying emotion was and how you could have dealt with it?
- Can you be brave enough to get back in touch with all of those underlying emotions that you've been hiding behind the angry MASK, even when it is hard to do so?
- Can you be brave enough to practice looking for the underlying emotion each time we put the angry MASK on, and can we be compassionate towards others when they are wearing the angry MASK and as ourselves "I wonder what their underlying emotion is?"
- Can we honestly answer the question of how we used the energy anger gave to us (constructively or destructively) and how we expressed ourselves when we were angry (In a way that helped the situation or in a way that made the situation worse?).

You have done a great job sticking with me so far…I hope what you've already read has begun to help you view your anger in a slightly different way, and that it has created a desire in you to deal with your underlying emotions directly through communicating and expressing how you feel as a way of using the angry MASK less and less…

We have a little farther to go on our journey---but the key to all of this is practicing the MASK theory—that is, find that underlying

emotion and deal the heck out of it by communicating and expressing your feelings!! (We need to communicate appropriately of course, and open up a respectful dialogue that employs "I" statements and a consideration of the other person's feelings as well)...I know you have it in you! Keep with me – we will make it to the end of our enlightenment!

Chapter Seven:

What do I do now?!

So now hopefully the next time something happens that creates a underlying emotion within you that may be in danger of being MASKED with anger, you might be asking yourself "What is my underlying emotion and how do I deal with it – how can I express myself by using "I" statements and creating a dialogue?"

But what if you succumb to human nature and put the angry MASK on before you can identify the underlying emotion? We're only human and it's going to happen, right? Absolutely! Don't beat yourself up over it—remember to use a Quick Response Strategy, give your brain a few minutes to adjust its thinking (remember Emotional thoughts and Intellectual thoughts?)...your QRS will help you to not act out in the hostile frame of mind, and hopefully avoid behaviors that you might regret—behaviors that bring with them negative consequences (like getting arrested, saying hurtful things or acting in hurtful ways that hurt relationships etc.).

So now you're standing there after using your QRS, and you're still feeling a little juiced and angry over the whole situation (whatever it was)...now what?

Using your QRS helped you not to bite off anyone's head, or kick in anyone's door, or smash someone's television set, but you still have all of this energy created by your anger (remember Chapter Four) and you have this need to express yourself. So now what??

Great question...sit tight, the answer is coming right now........

When you have put the angry MASK on, and you've done the responsible thing by using an QRS, chances are you still are going to act in some way to address whatever the situation was that contributed to you putting the MASK on in the first place...I call this the "four choices you can make when you are angry".

If you're saying to yourself right now that there are way more than four choices you can make when you're angry, give me a chance to explain and read on...

Just as anger is a choice, so is the way you can react to your anger a choice also...

So, let's recap the situation:

You have put the angry MASK on, used a strategy to get your thinking to a less hostile level...and now you feel the need to express your anger, and use some of that energy that anger has bestowed on you...Here are your choices:

You can choose to:
1. **Do Nothing**
2. **Be Hostile**
3. **Get Even** or
4. **Be Assertive**, and seek resolution to the issue that started everything in the first place!

Sounds pretty easy right? I mean, after all, there are only four choices to choose from, right? Well, it's not always that easy as you know…

Each choice brings with it its own consequences or results… predicting what those results might be is critical in choosing the best choice……

So how do you know which is the right choice to make at the time of your situation? It is tricky, but not *that* tricky…let's explore this some more with an example:

Let's say that you are at the movie theatre with your significant other…you sit down in your seats and get ready to enjoy the flick…

As the previews are rolling, you feel something push on the back of your seat, and it rocks you forward a bit….you glance back to see the guy behind you has his knees squarely on the back of your chair and with every movement he makes you are feeling a thrust into your spine…Needless to say it is irritating you a bit…Irritation is a low level of anger, and so you have this angry MASK on inside the movie theatre as the movie is about to start…

Let's use our flow chart to illustrate the situation described:

1. **Something happens**: The guy behind you is rocking your chair with his knees
2. **You feel an underlying emotion**: You may be thinking that the guy behind you is not being considerate…the fact that he is not considering your feelings may have you feeling frustrated, or disrespected…these are underlying emotions!
3. **These underlying emotions cause you some discomfort**: No one likes to feel as though their feelings are not being considered, and no one likes

to feel as though they are being disrespected—it is uncomfortable!

4. **You have a choice to deal with the underlying emotions or put on the angry MASK.**

In our example, you have initially put on the angry MASK and are feeling a bit irritated. Pretty normal, right? I agree, it could be irritating to have someone sitting behind you at the movies with their knees squarely on the back of your chair, pushing and rocking you every time they move. Remember from Chapter two? **Anger is normal**, so you are not a freak and not a bad person!

So, you take a few deep breaths and get your emotional thoughts under control (that's using a QRS!), but now it is time to act....What do you do? Scream for HELP? I am kidding—remember you have four choices....

But before you make any choice, let me ask you "What is your goal for the evening—what did you want to accomplish when you went to the movies?"

Most likely your goal was to enjoy the show. Now with this guy behind you, your goal is jeopardized. It's tough to enjoy the show when someone is rocking your chair.

So getting back to which of the four choices and which you are going to choose...

If you are generally a passive person and **choose to do nothing**, will the guy stop rocking your chair? Probably not. It will most likely continue, and you will most likely continue to be irritated.

If you **get hostile**, and become **aggressive** and turn around and threaten the guy with a glare and a tone of voice that implies "You better move your knees or else I will rearrange your face" there is a chance he will listen to you.....there is also a chance that he will invite

you out to the parking lot to settle your differences. This could result in the both of you being arrested!

If you choose to **get even** and take a passive/aggressive route (You could act like the movie scared you and launch your super mega gulp soda over your left shoulder and onto his lap). This might make you feel a whole lot better but it may only accomplish a temporary feeling of satisfaction. The guy behind you may feel the need to dump his super mega big gulp over the top of your head!

In all three of the instances mentioned thus far, none of them resulted in you enjoying the movie. That was your original goal, remember?

What I want you to try to remember in situations like these --- situations that are ripe for choosing the wrong actions--- is to predict what the likely outcomes will be if you act in each of the four choices, and see which one would bring you a consequence or result that most closely matches your goal…

In other words, ask yourself:

1. **"What will most likely happen if I do nothing?"**
   ANSWER: He will continue to rock my chair and I will remain irritated, and not enjoy the movie. THIS DOES NOT MATCH YOUR GOAL!

2. **"What will most likely happen if I get hostile?"**
   ANSWER: He will probably get hostile back and we may end up fighting. THIS DOES NOT MATCH YOUR GOAL!

3. **"What will most likely happen if I choose to get even?"**

ANSWER: He may retaliate and that could lead to an aggressive encounter (translation: it may end up in a fight!) THIS DOES NOT MATCH YOUR GOAL!

So what might happen if you are **assertive?** Assertive behavior is when you tell someone what you think, how you feel and what you want—in a non-threatening way. It is easy to tell someone what we want—and this might sound like this:

"Get your knees off of the back of my chair!"

If you have a threatening tone, this attempt at being assertive will most likely be interpreted by the guy sitting behind you at the movie theatre as a hostile act because it implies "Get your knees off of the back of my chair OR ELSE!" PLUS, you have only stated one of the three pillars of assertiveness—**what you want.**

It is important to state all three pillars:
1. What you think
2. How you feel
3. What you want

Why is this important to state all three?

You want to paint a picture for the person you are dealing with... letting them know where you're coming from. You don't want to leave any of your motivating factors up to their imagination.

In essence, what you are doing is saying: "This is why I am asking you to move your knees—no hidden macho agenda, I just want to enjoy the movie, and I am trying to be a decent guy—can you work with me?"

An assertive response may sound like this:

"I don't know if you realize this or not, but your knees are on the back of my chair, and every time you move I am getting rocked...I have to honest with you, I'm getting a little irritated. All I am trying

to do is enjoy the movie, do you think you could slide back in your chair a little please?"

If you can do this and do it in a non-threatening tone, you may be surprised at the level of cooperation you receive.

This approach, unlike the other three in this situation, provides a chance for resolution to the problem: His knees rocking your chair. It is no surprise that the word 'resolution' has the word **solution** within it!

Also if he stops rocking your chair, you can relax and enjoy the movie, and that was your goal in the first place!

Assertive behavior has some built in advantages:
1. It allows you to speak your mind—remember expressing yourself is a good thing—it gets things off of your chest.
2. It gives the person you're dealing with a chance to do the right thing—especially if you begin your assertive phrase with "**I don't know if you realize this or not…**" This phrase allows the person, even if they know they are doing something irritating (like rocking your chair at the movies), a chance to feign ignorance and gives them an opportunity to do the right thing without appearing like a bad person. It gives them an "out". By using the phrase "**I don't know if you realize this or not**" you are not saying that they are bad…you are saying that it is possible that he is rocking your chair by accident, and if it was accidental, no one is to blame and things can be put 'right' without anyone feeling badly about what happened.

There are no guarantees with assertive behavior though. You must be prepared for things not to work out as well…if the guy behind you tells you to go fly a kite, then what do you do?

Well, then you wipe the slate clean and start all over. Your first attempt at assertiveness did not produce resolution. But now you still have all of the four choices to at your disposal again---only this time you have more information about the guy sitting behind you...now you know that he is not cooperative, and that he may be aggressive.

Re-evaluate your goal...is it still possible to enjoy the movie sitting in front of this guy? Fight the urge to match his aggressiveness with your own, if you think it could get you into trouble...If your goal changes, (Remember your original goal was to enjoy the movie) pick one of the four choices to act that will bring about the closest match with what your new goal is...

Your new goal might be to not get in to a confrontation with the loser behind you. In this instance maybe moving your seats to another location might be the best decision. You could ratchet up the assertiveness and bring the movie usher into the equation. **You have options**—realize that. There are other ways of handling the situation besides defending your pride – remember anger makes it harder to think clearly, and if you act out in that unclear frame of mind you may make decisions with your "E" thoughts and bad things could result!

Let's review this section:

When you find yourself in a situation in which you have the angry MASK on, and you've used a QRS and are ready to act, you have four choices:
1. Do Nothing
2. Get Hostile
3. Get Even
4. Be ASSSERTIVE

Let your mind run through all of the possibilities of what the consequences or results would be if you acted in each of these ways,

and choose the way that you think will bring about the closest result that matches your goal.

It sounds easy, but trust me, when anger is messing with your ability to think clearly, choosing the best way to act can be very difficult...that is why the QRS is so important! Remember to use a **Strategy and shrink those emotional thoughts**!

CHAPTER EIGHT:

Let's wrap this puppy up and get out there and start applying the stuff you've learned!

Wow…you made it this far—good for you! I told you that I would stick with you the whole way! It is a lot of information to remember, and a lot to try to apply—but you can do it! We will review all of the important factors in this chapter, but before we do, I want to point out some things for you to remember and keep in mind: I call these **Pete's Twelve Commandments of Anger Management:**

1. **Everyone can change** things they don't like about themselves (like how they handle their anger) if they are motivated to do so.
2. **No one is perfect**. We all make mistakes. We all handle our anger in ways on occasion that we are not proud of—even me (and I wrote the book!). Try not to beat yourself up when this happens—try to learn from the experience instead.
3. **No one can change overnight**—it takes practice… Practice the MASK theory, looking for the underlying emotion, and then deal with it directly. Use your

strategies, make better choices of behavior…you won't be able to do it all the time, but practicing often will get you to the point of being as close to perfect as you can be.

4. **Give yourself credit** for trying—remember your self-talk---let it be the voice of support for you as you make the efforts to manage your anger in a more appropriate way…

5. If you feel comfortable in doing so, **share with your inner circle** of loved ones what you are trying to accomplish. Let them know that you are aware of your anger issues and that you are trying to work on them – elicit their help in the effort—a good support system can go a long way!

6. **Don't give up** if at first things don't seem to be working perfectly…remember that a long journey begins with the first step, and sometimes we have to take two steps backwards in order to accomplish one step forward.

7. **Be committed**. Change is not easy, giving up is. You can do this! But it will not happen on its own…you have to put in the effort—not just give the effort lip service. I know this sounds like tough love—I care about whether you are successful or not—I want this to work for you!

8. **Getting discouraged is normal**, just like getting angry is normal…you will feel discouraged at times—but don't lose sight of the progress (however large or small) that you are making…keep trying and keep practicing!

9. **Take notice** if people notice a difference in you…let yourself feel good about positive changes that are taking place! When we feel good about what we are doing, our self worth increases—and as a result we want to keep doing good things---this is a natural reinforcer!

10. **Accept and feel good about 'little victories'**…when you are able to express and deal directly with your underlying emotion, and you are able to open a dialogue

with someone instead of getting angry—that is a good thing! Recognize this even if the dialogue doesn't turn out exactly like you want it to...dialogue is better than anger!

11. **Be aware** that when you make changes in your behavior, it might take folks around you a bit of time to adjust to the 'new you'...Don't be caught off guard if people are a little skeptical of your new anger management style at the beginning...time will show them that you are for real!

12. **Review** the material often...out of sight is truly out of mind...keep this information fresh in your mind so that you can reference it quickly in your mind and actions when you need it!

Now let's review what you've learned...

• Anger is a normal emotion that everyone experiences... Anger is normal, the way some people react to their anger is not.

• Self-talk plays a large part in our ability to manage our anger. Self-talk can be supportive and calming or it can be negative and 'anger fueling'...What type of self talk do you most often have inside of your head? Is it helping you or hurting you? You control your self talk, and if you need to change it for the better, use the three R's: **Realize** the negative self talk, **Replace** the negative thoughts with more positive ones, and **Reinforce** the fact that you are trying –give yourself some credit!

Remember:

• What we think influences how we feel, and how we feel influences how we act....in other words we are what we think, basically.

- Anger is a secondary emotion that MASKS another emotion that comes first (underlying emotion)...If we can identify the underlying emotion and deal with it directly, then we do not need to put the angry MASK on at all...Identifying the underlying emotion requires us to be brutally honest with ourselves!

- Dealing with the underlying emotion directly requires communicating and expressing our feelings. This is extra difficult for men to do because we have been socialized to distance ourselves from our feelings...Communicating and expressing our feelings requires the use of 'emotional words' and the development of an emotional vocabulary . "I" statements also help in effectively communicating our feelings. "I" statements help us label our feelings, and they also help to reduce the defensiveness of the person we are communicating with.

- If you put the angry MASK on, use a Quick Response Strategy (QRS) to 'buy' your brain a little time to begin to start thinking more clearly before you take action... Anger stops us from thinking clearly...a QRS helps us to reduce the volume of our "E" thoughts and increase the volume of our "I" thoughts...This will lead to better decision making, and help avoid the types of behaviors that we later regret...

- Once you've used a QRS, then you still have to act in some way...choose the type of behavior from the four choices...What result would each behavior produce? Choose the behavior that would produce the outcome that most closely matches that of your goal for the situation...

Four Choices of behaviors:
1. Do Nothing
2. Get hostile

3. Get Even
4. Be Assertive

- Finally, follow the twelve commandments while trying to accomplish your goals of managing your anger more appropriately. Build a support network to help you in your efforts. Review the material often to keep the information fresh in your mind. Practice the MASK theory's principals every chance you get—dissect your anger every time you can and learn from each occurrence........and don't give up! You can do this!

Chapter Nine:

Points of reference:

I have arranged to give a brief bullet of the points, with a reference page to where in the book you can find more information...let this serve as your quick index for finding the information you need...

- **Anger** is a **normal emotion** (page 2)
- **Self-talk** can fuel more angry thoughts and feelings, or it can help calm us down—we control our self talk! (pages 5, 6)
- **Perceptions, hopes and expectations** are forms of self talk that we are in control of—if we perceive things in an angry way, or consistently expect too much of ourselves or those around us we may become angry as a result (page 7)
- We **cannot control other people** or their actions.... **we can control**, however the way we react to other people—we are ultimately responsible for what we do (pages 7, 8)
- Our **thoughts** influence how we **feel**, and how we feel influences how we **act**...therefore our thoughts are very important because they eventually determine to a large degree how we act or behave (page 5)

- The **MASK** theory states that anger is a secondary emotion. When something happens and we feel an underlying emotion, we often MASK this emotion with anger instead of dealing with it directly. (pages 11)
- **Anger flow chart** (page 23)
- **Quick Response Strategies** buy your brain time to allow your **"E" thoughts** a chance to shrink and your **"I" thoughts** time to get louder (pages 24, 25)
- Dealing directly with the **underlying emotion** through expressing and communicating our feelings (page 28)
- Building an **emotional vocabulary**, and using your 'emotional words' to express your feelings (page 30)
- **Expressing** your emotions and dealing directly with the underlying emotion reduces your need to use the angry MASK (page 31)
- Using **"I" statements** to help you effectively communicate your feelings (pages 33, 37)
- **Four choices** are Do Nothing, Get Hostile, Get Even and Be Assertive (pages 38, 39, 40, 41, 42, 43)
- **Twelve Commandments** of anger management (page 47)
- **One page "Bible"** of anger management (page 52)
- **Email Support: Peteangmgtman@aol.com** (page 34)
- **Testimonials** (page 55)

One Page "Bible" of anger management

1. Something Happens = An event takes place that gets the ball of emotions rolling
2. You feel an underlying emotion
3. Discomfort is felt
4. You have a choice: A) Identify and deal with the underlying emotion OR

            B) Put on the anger MASK
5. If you choose to put on the anger MASK, use a QRS (Quick Response Strategy) to help keep your emotional

thinking in check and to give your intellectual thinking a chance to be heard.

5A. If you have chosen to become angry or given in to your 'hot button', remember that there are 4 choices... Each choice brings with it their own consequences—be careful here! Aggressive, hostile behaviors can get you into trouble---and anger destroys relationships in the long run!

6. If you've chosen to deal directly with your underlying emotion (Good for you!!!), communicate your feelings by using "I" statements and your emotional vocabulary. Opening up dialogue with the person that you are angry with can actually make your relationship closer in the long run, and not only preserve the relationship but help make it stronger!

7. Use every opportunity in which anger is or has been present to learn from the experience...seek out and uncover that underlying emotion—even if you have to do it after your anger has already presented itself—this will prepare you for the next time that same underlying emotion arises.

8. Ask for help – solicit assistance from those close to you by asking them to point out the times when you are choosing anger over dialogue—this may be irritating at first—but helpful in the long run...

9. Be compassionate with yourself—you will make mistakes and you will continue to handle anger inappropriately at times...You are not perfect—don't expect to be—just be the best you can be!

10. Be compassionate with others—when you see them angry, don't immediately respond with your own anger or judgment---remember they have a underlying emotion under their MASK, seek it out and help them with dialoguing – you both will feel better for it!

Use the support number if you need to—that is what it is there for...

TESTIMONIALS:

I had the privilege of working with Pete personally when he first started teaching the principles of anger management. To be honest, I was somewhat skeptical at first. I thought that it would be a bunch of BS and that it would be a waste of time. I remember my first meeting with Pete – he was so enthusiastic about what he was teaching that it was kind of contagious—and I think it comes across in the pages of this book. He asked me to keep an open mind and to be honest with myself—and I was—and I am glad of it. Applying the principles he shared with me truly changed my outlook on anger and how I was managing it. I was embroiled in a bitter divorce, and was on my way to a stroke or heart attack because of the way I would let anger get the best of me. In particular, E and I thinking was what stuck with me the most—that is, besides Pete's engaging personality and zest for what he does…Read the book. Keep an open mind and be honest with yourself. Don't get discouraged—it works!

Art
Baltimore, MD

I participated in one of Pete's anger management workshops because I was court ordered after my boyfriend filed assault charges against me. This in itself was irritating to me because I had not assaulted my boyfriend – actually he was the one that assaulted me—but he was the one that called the police and filed the protective order—so I was the one with the charges against me. When the judge ordered me to complete an anger management program I thought, "What a bunch of _____!"

I attended Pete's workshop and told him the whole story. He was very understanding, and asked me to keep an open mind and to really try to apply the principles he taught to my life specifically. He reminded me that like with anything else in life you get out of it what you put into it. I still didn't think that I had a problem with anger management—but after learning about the MASK I realized that even I could improve my life by following the principles he taught and the ones that are in this book. I know it sounds corny to say "It was life changing"---but it was. I am happier, I like myself more, my self esteem is higher and I can recognize situations and react to them in a much more appropriate way—ways that I can feel good about. Get the book—read it—live it—you won't be sorry!

Sandra
Columbia, MD